# The Unofficial Disneyland Drinking Companion

## Christopher Schmidt

**Theme Park Press**
*The Happiest Books on Earth*
www.ThemeParkPress.com

Although every precaution has been taken to verify the accuracy of the information contained herein, no responsibility is assumed for any errors or omissions, and no liability is assumed for damages that may result from the use of this information.

Theme Park Press is not associated with the Walt Disney Company.

The views expressed in this book are those of the author and do not necessarily reflect the views of Theme Park Press.

Theme Park Press publishes its books in a variety of print and electronic formats. Some content that appears in one format may not appear in another.

Editor: Bob McLain

Layout: Artisanal Text

ISBN 978-1-68390-069-6

Printed in the United States of America

**Theme Park Press | www.ThemeParkPress.com**

Address queries to bob@themeparkpress.com

*For Tiffany, Gracey, and Jack,*
*and the passionate Disney spirit inside us all*

# Contents

# Author's Note

I hold a simultaneously vast and special place in my heart for all things Disney. I also have a bit of a fondness for savoring exotic beverages and craft beer upon sun-dappled patios. Where these two pleasures intersect, true happiness may be found. For every charming wine terrace that opens up at Disney California Adventure, every quick-service counter that serves IPA, every gift shop with a beverage cooler, the world becomes a better place.

This guide is an examination of an extraordinary extra layer of magic that lies on top of the already wonderful Disneyland Resort experience. Responsible adult enjoyment, handled in a responsible, adult manner, can be as memorable and fulfilling as any of the incredible moments you experienced throughout your own Disney history. It's entirely up to you how you're going to conduct yourself. With a positively scintillating margarita coursing through your system, please remain aware of the power you have to impact others' precious memories, even inadvertently. Enjoy yourself. Let others do so as well.

# Introduction

From day one, Walt Disney's dream was to create a place where adults and children could come have fun together. There's a plaque at the end of Main Street that says so. In the boardroom, where Walt's people first brainstormed this now-famous ambition, I doubt anyone suggested Disneyland also become a place to come and get drunk.

Disney is all about family. A passion for Mickey Mouse, the Magic Kingdom, and the Matterhorn is a trait that is handed down through generations of dedicated Disney guests. The glint in a child's eyes when they meet a real-life princess for the first time, pilot their first Dumbo, or don their first pair of mouse ears is what the dream is all about. A couple obnoxious "grownups" with substance abuse issues, and a misconception for what is expected of them, can leave a lasting scar on an impressionable child's otherwise happy memory. Please, don't be those people.

Whether visiting the Disneyland Resort as part of a family, or simply subjecting surrounding families to your own unavoidable influence, never lose sight of where you are. Be aware of the reason almost everyone else is there. From Walt's earliest glimmer of imagination, to the present day, no one's Disney dream entails or benefits from an interaction with drunken strangers.

Have fun. That is, and has always been, the point. If enjoying yourself involves becoming a public spectacle, please consider a more suitable venue; perhaps somewhere with a lower frequency of children, and people with less-childlike enthusiasms.

Having an exotically assembled beverage, rare vintage wine, and a refreshing, flavorful micro-brew, while immersed in theme-park paradise, is a life affirming experience. Do it. You are meant to. Disney wouldn't offer alcohol otherwise. Just, please, pace yourself. If we, as adults, demonstrate we can be trusted to consume responsibly, one day these adult beverages may not be so prohibitively expensive, or at least not served in neon bright cups of shame.

What follows is a complete listing of every Disneyland Resort restaurant, bar, kiosk, and quick-service counter where you may find and purchase select alcoholic beverages. The beer, wine, and cocktails indicated are available at press time. Of course, that's subject to change at Disney's discretion, and change it does, often. If you risk missing your Soarin' FastPass window to get yourself a Racer 5 IPA from the Alfresco Terrace, we admire your enthusiasm, though apologize in advance if it is no longer sold there.

Beer and wine varieties are listed by location. For bars and restaurants serving a full complement of liquor and offering an extensive wine list, it would be overly cumbersome to list them all. Select wines and specialty beverages are detailed for your contemplation and potential enjoyment.

Disneyland Resort draft beer is most often delivered in a 16-ounce plastic cup, especially at Disney California Adventure, where no one wants you tooling around with a glass bottle in your hands. 12-ounce bottles are available at non-Disney California Adventure bars, some restaurants, and gift shops.

Since Disney changes its prices so often, we don't include prices in this guide. The more you drink, the less you'll notice the prices, anyway.

# CHAPTER ONE

# Drinking at Disney California Adventure

Every worthwhile examination of the Disneyland Resort begins, ends, and revolves around Disneyland itself. This does not apply when discussing Disney-fashioned drinking spots. With the exception of Club 33, which is closed to mere mortals, Disneyland is rather a difficult place to get a proper drink. With seventeen Disney-themed beer, wine, and booze dispensaries, Disney California Adventure, then, is the resort's first choice in adult refreshment.

Disney California Adventure makes copious use of the 16-ounce neon yellow cups, mentioned previously. While this does help mark potential problem individuals, it's more likely a deterrent for underage drinking. What it positively does is keep you from sneaking beer into Disneyland. Shame on you if you even think of trying this. Cast members at the park gate could, perhaps, be a little more understanding when someone unwittingly arrives at their turnstile with one of these cups in their hand. There is every chance this person was simply savoring their drink rather than attempting to perpetrate an unforgivable Disney offense. That said, I'm sorry. I am committed to never doing it again.

Keeping with the theme, charm, and Disney-authentic attention to detail, many representative Disney California Adventure breweries, wineries, and beverage offerings are true California natives. While I wholly support guests who opt for a glass of French wine or Scotch, I cannot forgive anyone who chooses a Bud Light over a California-crafted IPA. This is no slight on the fine people at Anheuser-Busch. Bud Light was served at my wedding. I didn't drink any, but it was there for those who insisted upon it. At a rigidly themed amusement park, a choice between a Sam Adams and a lovingly crafted California brew is no choice at all. If you plan to drink beer during your visit, do yourself, your taste buds, and your sense of sophistication a favor: keep it local.

## Alfresco Tasting Terrace

*Pacific Wharf*
*Serves: Wine, Beer (12oz), Small Bites*

Even if we weren't proceeding alphabetically, this venue could well appear at the top of our list. For a theme park, Alfresco is unexpectedly refined. There's an impressive wine list. A couple IPAs. Elegant wine-country theming. A bird's eye view of the park. Alfresco Terrace is an attraction all its own.

Seating is limited, and the hours are sporadic. And it's a little off the path (up a flight of stairs). When it is open, it's often easier to get a seat here than at the more obvious Mendocino wine bar out front.

Not a ton of items on the food menu, but what they have is divine. The charcuterie is unlike anything you'd expect to find at a park that also sells corn dogs. If you haven't experimented, IPA pairs with pretty much every available cheese.

The wine list is as impressive as it is vast, and you can buy wine here by the glass or by the bottle. A bottle of wine is a significant amount of alcohol to have in your possession all at once at an amusement park. Drinking wine by the bottle, while surrounded by roller coasters and Pixar parades, it can be easy to lose track of how much you have had. If your sommelier sells you a bottle of Dasani, when you didn't ask for it, it's a pretty fair indication you need to slow down.

***Disney Drinking Tip.*** Dumping wine from its bottle into a water bottle is not a ground-breakingly clever way to bootleg booze into unauthorized sections of the resort. Disney security is well aware of the practice. Expect a visit from the kindly cast members in the white hats if you attempt to leave Disney California Adventure with open bottles of Malbec-tinted Dasani. Count on a more hasty, deservedly less amicable encounter, if your party chooses to stage wine-filled-water-bottle boat races in line for Mater's Junkyard Jamboree. There are kids everywhere. Disney would rather not have them influenced by foolishness and colorful language. If you find yourself on the wrong end of a confrontation with Disney security, know that you absolutely asked for it. They are happy to interact with guests, but they'd just as soon keep it amicable. Most often, they are there to save the misbehaving from themselves. Try to limit the negative encounters. Having a $110 bottle of Pinot taken away from you on Heimlich's Chew Chew Train might well make for an interesting story, if by interesting you mean disgraceful.

### What's to Drink

- Disney Family of Wines, white/red/rosé flights, 2oz tasters
- Wine by the glass
- Wine by the bottle
- Zonin Prosecco, Italian Sparkling
- Racer 5 IPA
- Hangar 24 Orange Wheat
- Anaheim Hefeweizen
- Blue Moon
- Corona
- Heineken
- Bud Light
- Samuel Adams Seasonal

# Ariel's Grotto

*Paradise Pier*
*Serves: Beer, Wine, Full Bar, Breakfast, Lunch,*
*Dinner, Specialty Drinks Menu*

There are people in this world who cannot imagine drinking alcohol in a Disney-designed character restaurant for children. These highly discriminating individuals are easy to identify; they don't have any children of their own. For those in the know, those whose kids have been all over them for months to see Elsa, Belle, and Tiana, nothing pairs more perfectly with an early morning Disney princess parade than an Absolut Bloody Mary. Fortunately, high-ranking Disney decision-makers agree and understand the pressing needs of bedraggled parents.

Reservations are all but required at Ariel's, and they expect you to order a meal. It's better if you also have at least one child in tow. So, you probably aren't going to simply drop in for a drink. Given its nature, and all the impressionable children everywhere, that's probably for the best. If you are compelled to go anyway, say, due to your desperate need for good World of Color seats, take solace in the full bar—just try not to take too much advantage of it.

## *Featured Cocktails*

### Magical Star Cocktail
*X-Fusion Organic Mango and Passion Fruit Liqueur, Parrot Bay Coconut Rum, Pineapple Juice, and a souvenir multi-colored Glow Cube*

### Spicy Watermelon Margarita
*Patrón Silver Tequila, Habanero Lime, Watermelon, and fresh Lime Juice*

### Moscow Mule
*Russian Standard Vodka, fresh Lime Juice, and Agave Nectar topped with Ginger Beer*

### Rye Manhattan
*Bulleit Rye Small Batch American Whiskey, Carpano Antica Sweet Vermouth, and Angostura bitters, garnished with Luxardo Gourmet Maraschino Cherries*

## *Featured Brews (all 16oz draft)*

- Anchor Steam
- Karl Strauss Red Trolley Ale
- Karl Strauss Tower 10 IPA
- Blue Moon
- Bear Republic Racer 5 IPA
- Anchor California Lager

# Award Wieners

*Hollywood Land*
*Serves: Beer, Quick Service Lunch & Dinner*

Regarding adult beverages, this classic walk-up-window eatery offers one lone beer. Still, this places it convincingly above every establishment that has fewer. The present selection is Karl Strauss Red Trolley Ale. As a San Diego native, I am particular to Karl Strauss, and Red Trolley is a fine example of its variety, though I much favor Karl's fine line of IPAs. Blessedly, those are available all over the park. Not here, unfortunately, but almost everywhere else.

If you're at this end of the park, or anywhere near the Disney California Adventure entrance, and you just want a beer, this is an easy way to get it. You would do well to keep this and similar beer-dispensing quick-service counters in mind. Time is often of the essence within the Disneyland Resort. Whether pressed by a swiftly closing FASTPASS window, or hustling to meet friends or accommodate family, opportunities to efficiently grab a beverage are not to be squandered. A proper awareness of the park can be the difference between enjoyment of a craft beer and frustration in a line somewhere (see Cove Bar).

Despite a limited selection, Award Wieners is a hidden gem for those who favor a drink at the park, though may be traveling with people who do not. It's close to the main gate, and thus easy to reach. It is directly across Hollywood Blvd from a restroom. If you cannot get away from the overly judgmental members of your party (do not ditch your family), perhaps you can distract them with a restroom break.

### What's to Drink

- Karl Strauss Red Trolley Ale (16oz draft)

# Bayside Brews

*Paradise Pier*
*Serves: Beer, Quick bites*

Another fairly low-frills quick-service counter, Bayside Brews is a glorious oasis for the thirsty theme park patron. Many restaurants, carts, and service counters are fraught with an overabundance of distracting food and drink items. This can render an otherwise convenient beverage outlet prohibitively busy. Not Bayside. Bayside specializes in and is thoroughly committed to its craft. Despite being relegated to a distant corner of the park, it's a splendid place to go for a beer.

All of Bayside's brews are on draft; even the Bud Light. This doesn't mean you should order a Bud Light (unless they're out of everything else). If the Karl Strauss seasonal tap beer happens to be Aurora Hoppyalis, as it is currently, that's what you should get.

It's a bit of a hike to get here from most other areas of the resort. It's worth it. The area through which you walk is as inspiring as the beer waiting for you when you arrive. If family pressure dictates you settle for a Dos Equis on the wharf, you could do worse. But don't cheat yourself due to logistics or laziness. A few extra furlongs is worth finding no line and better beer at Bayside.

## *What's to Drink (all 16oz draft)*

- Karl Strauss Tower 10 IPA
- Karl Strauss Seasonal
- Sierra Nevada Pale Ale
- Blue Moon
- Pacifico Cerveza
- Bud Light

# Boardwalk Pizza & Pasta

*Paradise Pier*
*Serves: Beer, Sangria, Lunch, Dinner*

Disney California Adventure is delightfully loaded with outdoor dining options. Paradise Pier is the arguable patio-seating capital. Between Bayside Brews and the Boardwalk you will find a vast expanse of open tables, offering every desired level of sun and elemental exposure.

Boardwalk Pizza, and neighboring Paradise Garden Grill (below), offer a variety of moderate to truly healthy dining options. A salad or grilled chicken is all the justification you need to then guiltlessly enjoy a full-bodied Karl Strauss out in the open air. A charming gazebo is the plaza's crown jewel, where live entertainment may be found throughout the day and evening. If you like the idea of live music, beer, and sunshine, then we could be friends, and this is where we would hang out.

### What's to Drink

- Karl Strauss Seasonal (16oz draft)
- Bud Light (16oz draft)
- Red Sangria (on the rocks)

*Disney Drinking Tip, for Parents.* Paradise Pier houses a fair number of all-age attractions; meaning rides suitable for small children. Never, never, never abandon your kids, for any reason. If you have proper coverage, this is an opportune spot for one member of your party to slip over and grab a couple beers. Responsibility dictates you leave the most trustworthy adult to safeguard your offspring. Per Disney policy, however, guests are allowed only two adult beverages in a single purchase, with valid ID. If your co-parent is more likely to purchase two drinks for themselves, while you are stuck chaperoning on Goofy's Sky School, then perhaps *you* should make the beer run.

# Carthay Circle Lounge and Restaurant

*Buena Vista Street*
*Serves: Beer, Wine, Full Bar, Lunch, Dinner,*
*Select Specialty Drinks Menu available*

When Disney constructs a restaurant, instead of leaving it to, say, Wolfgang Puck's people, Carthay Circle is what you get. Charm, character, authenticity—as far as you know—and good old-fashioned attention to Disney detail. It's the type of place you are thrilled just to stand within and witness, much less eat and drink in. Still, you'll want to do that, too.

Visiting families are wholly welcome to enjoy food and age-appropriate refreshment in this and every Disney establishment. As a former bartender, I implore guests with an excess of, or with any particularly attention-starved children, to proceed directly into the restaurant. Or, perhaps you might consider grabbing a hotdog at Award Wieners on your way over to "a bug's land"?

Yes, Disney is all about family. Kids are rightly welcome everywhere within the resort. Surrounded by several sprawling miles of fun park, there are many alternatives to planting your brood in one of the few spots designed specifically for grownups (see, also, Trader Sam's). There is an entire kid's menu available in Carthay's lounge, so it's difficult to fault anyone for eating there as a family. Oh, except for all the people with IDs and withdrawal issues who can't get in because you took the last table.

The setting is 100% impeccable, old-world Disney. Guests gravitate toward it like an attraction, especially the lounge. It can be difficult to get a table, even if isn't full of families not heeding our advice. The elegant Golden-Era "theater" is well worth seeing, though whether it's worth the wait is debatable, when there's a line out the door. I love Carthay. I love Trader Sam's, Blue Bayou Restaurant, etc. Still, regardless of the enticing setting and scenery, I will not sacrifice a significant percentage of my park time for a meal, given the vast availability of food throughout the resort. Waiting ought to be reserved for E-ticket attractions and experiences similarly difficult to replicate; not gin cocktails and flatbread.

Beer and wine are available; indeed a fine selection of each. Yet, Carthay Circle is one of those ideal cocktail venues. Martinis aren't necessarily my thing, but here, surrounded by history and culture, is where you should have one. Legend has it the Scotch Mist was Walt Disney's drink of choice.

I am a wholly committed tippler, obviously. Yet, it's difficult to imagine Walt, a childhood hero, having a favorite type of drink. I can sooner picture Santa Claus with a scotch than Walt Disney. Not a criticism in the slightest, it's just hard to picture. That said, I would have killed to have a drink with the man. Imagine, after hours, the park completely shut down, sharing a cocktail and private moment with Walt Disney in that office above the fire depot, or on a bench outside the Main Street railroad station.

If you object to cocktails, do the folks waiting outside a solid. Snap a couple photos, grab those noisy kids in the corner who couldn't care less about the sentiment covering every wall, and make your way to a less specific locale. The guests outside want cocktails and Carthay-fashioned nostalgia. You can get whatever you and your kids prefer pretty much everywhere else.

If your server or bartender isn't overtly busy—it happens sometimes—request a Wildberry Lemonade (from the non-alcoholic beverages menu) with either your favorite gin or vodka. However you get it, it is the second best drink available in the park (see Fillmore's Pomegranate Limeade, below).

If you mistakenly enter through the set of doors on the right, you will come face-to-face with another bit of Disney exclusivity. Club 33 has a new Disney California Adventure annex, the 1901 Lounge, and I'm not sure why they don't keep that door locked. I blundered in there recently, thinking I was heading for the Carthay Lounge. I encountered a glorious, wholly unfamiliar lobby, and an exceedingly understanding cast member. He knew I was in the wrong place, but rather than embarrass us both, he greeted me as if I wasn't treading, unwittingly, on sacred ground. Knowing instinctively I was there by accident, he gave me a chance to present my membership, which he, I, and the leaded glass knew was not forthcoming. He remained polite, even empathetic, as I made my humble retreat. If what is beyond that check-in desk is as delightful as the people who run it, I want in.

## *Featured Cocktails*

### Carthay Martini
*Hendrick's Gin or Double Cross Vodka, Lillet Blanc Dry Vermouth, and Gourmet Truffle Olives served with an ice sphere*

### Ernest's Daiquiri
*Bacardi Superior Rum, Luxardo Maraschino Liqueur, fresh Lime and Grapefruit Juice, and Organic Agave Nectar, served up*

### The Derby
*Bulleit Bourbon, fresh Grapefruit Juice, and Honey, served up*

### Carthay Club Mojito
*Bacardi Superior Rum, Organic Mint from local farms, fresh Lime Juice, and Organic Agave Nectar topped with locally sourced purified sparkling water*

Pimm's Punch
*Pimm's No. 1 Liqueur, Plymouth Gin, Strawberry, and Lemonade*

## Featured Brews (all 16oz draft)

- Karl Strauss Tower 10 IPA (San Diego)
- Ballast Point Sculpin (San Diego)
- Hangar 24 Orange Wheat Ale (Redlands)
- North Coast Pranquster (Fort Bragg)

**Disney Drinking Tip.** The taps at many Disney dining establishments are rotary in nature, thus subject to change. During one visit, when my server regretfully informed me they were not currently pouring Tower 10, I panicked and almost ordered a wheat beer. Fortunately, a Sculpin tap is recognizable, even from across a darkly lit, turn-of-the-twentieth-century lounge.

Do not commit exclusively to the menu. They are compiled through significant time, effort, and expense. It is impossible to update them every time a keg changes. Take a gander behind the bar, or ask a cast member about anything new or different. As for the latter, I am terrible at that. To my detriment, I often settle for something I don't necessarily favor rather than risk what I perceive as an imposition. No committed Disney cast member will ever make you feel that your time and concerns are not of the utmost importance. Here, in Toontown, or at the front gate, strike up a conversation with a Disney cast member. They are there for you, and are categorically wonderful people. Do try to make sure you aren't holding up a line, or bending the ear of the one server in a room full of thirsty patrons, but get to know them when you can. Cast members are as integral to the magical experience as Sleeping Beauty Castle, the sparkle upon every metallic fixture, and the music in the air.

# Cocina Cucamonga Mexican Grill

*Pacific Wharf*
*Serves: Beer, Sangria, Quick Service Mexican food*

For any living in the Disneyland area, or the Southwest generally, theme park Mexican food is as underwhelming as you would expect. Cocina Cucamonga is alright. It's deceptively healthy, at least as it compares to corn dogs and hamburgers. You're probably not going to come all the way into the park just to eat here.

This is not the place to go for beer, either. At least not Cucamonga, specifically. They do serve beer, which is bueno. Your choices are Dos Equis and Tecate. Bueno again, for keeping to the theme, but I can think of a marinero's dozen Mexican brands that are better, and only a couple that aren't.

Dos Equis does run rather an effective ad campaign, but it's a beer you buy mostly because it's cheap. Yes, $7.25 (at press time) represents a discount for a Disney drink, and with the often prohibitive line at the adjacent Karl Strauss Beer Truck, you may be tempted to give the Cocina a go.

Instead, I recommend you grab a margarita or Sapporo from one of the other wharf establishments, then get in the Karl Strauss line anyway. If you absolutely must have a Mexican beer, Paradise Garden Grill, on the Pier, sometimes serves Negra Modelo. The difference in quality and taste is well worth the risk and moderate walk.

### What's to Drink
- Dos Equis Amber (16oz draft)
- Tecate (16oz draft)
- Red Sangria (on the rocks)

## Cove Bar
*Paradise Pier*
*Serves: Beer, Wine, Full bar, Artisan*
*Appetizers, Specialty Drinks menu*

This was once the most ideal and enviable place within the Disneyland Resort to enjoy a drink, aside from the Disneyland Hotel pool. Recently, the Cove Bar's location, offerings, and reputation have made it a difficult place to even sit down. Once upon a time you could walk straight into the bar, take your pick of tables, and delight in the beautiful weather and view. A server would be around shortly, and within minutes you'd be neck deep in craft brew, mixed drinks, and lobster-nacho euphoria.

The drinks, view, and limited menu are still exceptional. Watching from the wrong side of the host station, as every table stands resolutely occupied, compels one to long for forgotten days. The service is still wonderful. The poor kids are just overwhelmed. Cove Bar quietly absorbed the adjacent character greeting patio-gazebo to accommodate the inexorable rise in popularity. This has mostly served to further overwhelm the kitchen and cast members.

If you are fortunate enough to have a table, consider yourself blessed, even if you had to wait a while for it. Please be patient, service can seem slow. It's only because the Cove Bar patio is now so jammed with tables. Disney would prefer to have you sitting down in their restaurant rather than walking away from a frustrating line. Tragedy is, the line forms anyway. Sit back, enjoy the view, lagoon, and roller-coaster-strewn environs. By the time your drink arrives, you ought to have an appreciation for why you came to this sun dappled haven.

If you are going to linger—when the weather's right, you will be powerless not to—be sure to keep ordering stuff. You owe it to your server, and the people in line, to spend money or ship out. I am not proud of the person I have become, but when there's a line, combined with tables of guests treating this glorious bar like a park bench, I can almost see myself hurling complete strangers bodily into Paradise Bay.

If you happen by while there is no line, there are few better places to take in a meal, beverage, and a few peaceful moments. Get here at high tide, which seems to be all too often now, and you may be better off navigating toward calmer waters. I'm not trying to discourage anyone, but I would just love to see one of my favorite spots a little less inaccessible. So, yeah, I guess I am trying to discourage some of you.

Another semi-secret Cove Bar specialty drink has recently surfaced. You have likely noticed, if you've been anywhere near Paradise Pier in the last couple years. It's a bit of an eye-catcher. It's called Mickey's Fun Wheel Cocktail, and it's more glorious and inviting than an empty California Screamin' queue. If someone in the Cove Bar has one, you can see it from halfway across the park. A bright rainbow-beacon of flavor, Fun Wheel is not on the regular menu, and does not appear on the website. Once a knowing guest gets one on their table, there will shortly be twenty more throughout the bar. You don't even need to know what's in it—I'm gonna tell you, don't worry—when you see it, you want one.

Hypnotic, multilayered beauty, like an Amazonian tree frog, the signature markings ought to serve as a warning. This drink is sweet and strong. You better love both, or you won't want this. You're still going to order one, as soon as someone else does, but your body won't welcome it. It contains pineapple juice, passion-fruit vodka, rum, gin, and about half a hurricane glass of blue curaçao. If you manage to finish one of these, I recommend for your next act, you go ride Toy Story Midway Mania! There will surely be a line, and I think you could use the time letting your system balance itself.

## Featured Cocktails

### Raspberry-Ginger "Vojito"
*Finlandia Raspberry Vodka, Ginger, Mint, Raspberry Purée, and fresh Lime Juice topped with Coconut Water*

### Agave Nectar Margarita
*Tres Generaciones Organic Plata Tequila, Agave Nectar, and fresh Lime Juice*

### Ultimate Long Island Iced Tea
*Bacardi Superior Rum, Tito's Handmade Vodka, Hendrick's Gin, Cointreau, and Sweet-and-Sour with a splash of Coca-Cola*

### Moscow Mule
*Russian Standard Vodka, fresh Lime Juice, and Agave Nectar topped with Ginger Beer*

## Featured Brews (all 16oz draft)

- Karl Strauss Mosaic Session IPA (San Diego)
- Anchor Brewing Co. California Lager (San Francisco)
- Bear Republic Racer 5 IPA (Healdsburg)

# Cozy Cone Motel

*Cars Land*
*Serves: Specialty Drinks, Quick Bites, Soft Drinks*

There is a champagne bar at the top of the Eiffel Tower, in Paris. I think there is one in Las Vegas, too, but I'm talking about the original. If you've had the opportunity to enjoy a glass of bubbly on top of the world's most romantic observation tower, then you are familiar with what bliss feels like. At Walt Disney World you may replicate the mood and emotion at the France Pavilion in Epcot. The Grand Marnier Orange Slush embraces the French spirit orally and spiritually. If you get one, and simply drink it where you stand, you will have had a wonderful day.

In California, Disney California Adventure, to be specific, you may capture similar magic in a glass via Fillmore's Pomegranate Limeade. You get them in the center cone of the positively charming Cozy Cone Motel food court, in Cars Land. It is a most unlikely spot to find the best drink you've ever tasted. The Chili Cone Queso walkup window—yeah, I know— serves Fillmore's Fuelin' Groovy Ades. Available in two varieties, you would be foolish to not order the Pomegranate Limeade. I am sure the plain lemonade is also wonderful. I've never tried it (see foolish, above).

Oh, yeah, I'm recommending the one with vodka in it. If you've come this far into the book, you likely already knew that. I just wanna be sure. The drink used contain SKYY Vodka; I'm not sure what it is now. I am hesitant to ask those sorts of questions, because then attentive cast members start asking questions of their own. Then they start limiting the number of drinks in your possession, and before you know it there is an obvious number of people in white hats in the area. Drink responsibly, but have at least one of these. They're top-of-the-Eiffel-Tower amazing.

I like to take my cup of frozen deliciousness over to gawk at Luigi's Rollickin' Roadsters. They won't let you take it on the ride (all the more reason to get one). As much respect and admiration as I have for Disney Imagineers, interest in this attraction escapes me. What's most confounding is how Luigi's, in its current state, is meant to be an improvement on the ride it replaced. Sipping pomegranate-flavored happiness, I try to remember just how un-rideable Luigi's Flying Tires must have been.

In the middle distance, to my left, the Hollywood Tower of Terror façade stands shrouded in girders and scrim. I have full faith in the impending Guardians of the Galaxy makeover. As I glance back and see underwhelmed guests exiting Luigi's, a shred of doubt creeps into my brain. Well, doubt or frozen lemonade. Either way it gives me pause.

### What's to Drink

- Vodka and Pomegranate Limeade
- Vodka and all-natural Lemonade

# Flo's V8 Café

*Cars Land*
*Serves: Beer, Wine, Breakfast, Lunch, Dinner*

I incessantly sing the praises of the charming creation that is Cars Land, but the Imagineers really earned their authenticity badges here. The entire area makes you feel like you are in the middle of *Cars*, the movie; especially at night. At the intersection with the flashing yellow light, in front of Flo's Café, you will marvel at how humans could create anything so surreal.

Stand here long enough, and a DJ dance party will break out behind you. Traveling with others? Take advantage of this distraction and head into Flo's for a Racer 5 IPA. Popping into a café while they enjoy an impromptu street fair hardly qualifies as abandonment, so, go ahead.

Flo's is also your go-to when the Karl Strauss Beer Truck line proves intolerable. It's just around the bend from the wharf. From the tail end of the beer truck line you can see Flo's and practically place an order from there. Flo's draws a crowd, also, but they have more registers to serve you. The person taking your order is also not charged with drawing your beer. You would not believe how much this one extra responsibility can slow the process over at the beer truck.

As an added bonus, Flo's Café opens when the park does. Aside from the character breakfasts, Earl of Sandwich, and a couple of the resort hotel gift shops, this will be your earliest opportunity to get an adult beverage.

The crossroads outside Flo's is an incredible picture spot. Whether facing the red sandstone arch and waterfall, Ornament Valley, up or down Route 66, or back at Flo's itself, everywhere you look is an Instagram post waiting to be captured. Purchasing a plastic cup full of beer does not necessarily lend itself to turning complete circles, in the middle of this habitually busy intersection, taking one-handed pictures with your phone. I recommend taking photos first. Or, heaven forbid, set your drink down. I, of course, didn't think to do either, and apologize to the family I sort of spilled on.

### *What's to Drink*

- Racer 5 IPA (16oz draft)
- Grand-Am Pale Ale (16oz draft)
- Byron Chardonnay
- Fess Parker Riesling
- Chalone Pinot Noir
- Red Sangria (on the rocks)

# Ghirardelli Soda Fountain and Chocolate Shop

*Pacific Wharf*
*Serves: creative desserts that would make Walt Disney proud*

You will not find adult-specific beverages at Ghirardelli. If anyone in your group faults you for forgoing a beer in favor of a Sea Salt Caramel Quake Shake, find a new group. Better, link up with a group that will let you have both.

# Lucky Fortune Cookery

*Pacific Wharf*
*Serves: Beer, Lunch, Dinner*

A convenient and healthy option if you are looking for something other than pizza and French fries. I can't really recommend this quick-service counter for beer unless you love

Sapporo, or you came to the wharf to get a Karl Strauss, and are now facing an outrageous line.

Rather than leave the area, try a prestigious Japanese beer. With it, you can sit and enjoy the open-air splendor, walk somewhere else in the park that has something you prefer, or get in the beer truck line, which is what you really wanted anyway. Buying a beer just to take with you into another line to buy beer may not sound like the most Disney activity ever, but the Pacific Wharf patio can clearly support a second craft beer truck, and it's not our fault they haven't brought one in.

Honorable mention goes to Lucky Fortune Tea. Disney is doing some enticingly creative stuff with flavored foams in their beverages. This, unfortunately, is exclusively a non-alcoholic offering, but it is still wonderful. It's sweet. Like, really sweet. If you prefer plain tea, this ain't it.

### *What's to Drink*

- Sapporo (16oz draft)

# Mendocino Terrace

*Pacific Wharf*
*Serves: Beer, Wine, Quick Bites*

Similar to, and indeed just a staircase away from, the Alfresco Tasting Terrace, this sylvan patio is rivaled only by the Cove Bar for charm, ambiance, and people-watching perspective. Where Alfresco is an ideal, semi-private getaway, Mendocino allows guests to remain within the park's enthusiastically beating pulse. This is yet another incredible place to hang out for a bit with an indulgent beverage. Securing a table can be tricky.

Whichever parade currently courses through Disney California Adventure, this is unquestionably the best place to watch it. This doesn't completely mesh with what is Mendocino's primary purpose: to provide a relaxing, wine-savoring escape. Oh, if you time it right, you may absolutely have wine and watch the parade. But, between frolicking Pixar characters and the keen families who are also aware of the terrace's terrific vantage point, Mendocino is not always as peaceful as you might prefer.

Every sommelier cast member is wonderful, and it appears we're calling them "wine ambassadors" now. If you get Elizabeth, you are extra fortunate. She is true Disney nobility. Don't hold up the line to get her, certainly, though simply being in her presence for the few brief moments of your tasting might be worth letting others go ahead of you. Elizabeth is like your favorite aunt; a scintillating conversationalist, who knows a ton about wine. Except, Elizabeth is an improvement, since she isn't drinking, and doesn't start talking a little too loudly the way your aunt does when there's an open Shiraz in the room

As with the other wine terraces, the beverage list is lavish and lengthy. Terrace beer comes as a 12oz serving from a bottle. No, you don't get the bottle. Guests paying close attention already realize 12 ounces of beer from a bottle costs only 25 cents less than a comparable 16oz draft. The truly discriminating will understand that, with every draught, you essentially get four extra ounces of beer for a quarter. It means walking either to Flo's or the Karl Strauss Beer Truck. If you're committed to beer, it's worth the extra trip. Don't lament the splitting up of your party. They'll have their own line in which to wait. It's not like you're ditching them on an attraction. If you do go the Karl Strauss route, your line will likely be longer than that of the wine terrace. That's fine, too. It will give your group more time to locate an elusive table.

## What's to Drink

- White, Red, and Rosé Flights, 2oz-tasters
- Wine by the glass
- Wine by the bottle
- Piccini Prosecco, Italian Sparkling
- Warsteiner German Pilsner (12oz bottle)
- Anaheim Hefeweizen (12oz bottle)
- Blue Moon (12oz bottle)
- Corona (12oz bottle)
- Bud Light (12oz bottle)
- Samuel Adams Hopscape (12oz bottle)

***Disney Drinking Tip.*** Light beer appears throughout the resort with blatant regularity, a concession to those who don't truly like the taste of beer, or simply prefer not to have sixteen ounces of high-viscosity beverage coursing through their system as they ride roller coasters. I understand the place for light beer, I just believe that place to be a tailgate party or your uncle's table at your wedding reception. Were I mistaken, there would be a truck in Disney California Adventure dedicated to Budweiser products, and there'd be a line.

# Pacific Wharf Distribution Co.
*Pacific Wharf*
*Serves: Incredible Beer, Pretzels*

Only recently appearing on the park map, and not even listed on the dining tab of the Disneyland Resort website, at press time, this scantily promoted beer outlet is one of the resort's more popular attractions. Lovingly known as the Karl Strauss Beer Truck, its following puts Flik's, Luigi's, and Ariel's combined adventures to shame. Rivaling, often exceeding, crowds anywhere else in the park, the 12-tap craft beer walk-up counter warrants its own FASTPASS queue.

If you have even the slightest interest in truly well-made beer, become familiar with San-Diego-born Karl Strauss brewing. At any given time, Pacific Wharf has six varieties to suit most tastes and preferences. You won't find a pure light beer here. For that you can skulk over to Cocina Cucamonga or Lucky's Fortune Cookery, while your friends consume and cherish fountains of lovingly crafted brew.

Karl Strauss Tower 10 IPA has been served at the beer truck since shortly after it became available to the adoring public. Along with erecting the Matterhorn, procuring Star Wars, and repeatedly casting John Ratzenberger, such decisions are a measure of Disney's signature cleverness and brilliance. If you like IPA, you will love Tower 10. If you don't, get yourself into a position where you do. Your world will be the better for it. That such an amazing substance can be acquired and enjoyed within a Disney park in southern California represents a near-perfect confluence of my personal interests.

Tower 10 has recently given way at this location to new Karl Strauss standout Aurora Hoppyalis. It is an American style IPA that arouses within me blasphemous impulses. I think I like it better than Tower 10. I know! Try one, or two—adults are allowed to get two drinks at a time. See if I'm not mistaken.

Part of the beauty of the beer truck is its central location. Once you get through the unfortunate line—I'm old enough to remember when they didn't have to put stanchions out— you have a few excellent options. You may sidle over to one of the many available tables and enjoy your excellent beer in the beautiful wharf-replicated setting and sunshine. At lunchtime, during Disney's peak season, is about the only time this seating area fills up. You don't want to hang out here then, anyway. The hordes of kids illegally feeding the ducks, while their negligent parents strew trash in your personal space, can tarnish even the most pleasant of beer-relishing experiences.

Another equally wonderful option is to take your beer and head through the sandstone arch to Cars Land. Sip glorious ale in the presence of the latest Disney-fashioned creativity. Marvel at the landscape and wholly novel Radiator Springs Racers attraction. Contemplate what type of person is willing to spend an extra thirty to one-hundred minutes in the Racers' standby line. Considering I often lament the five minutes it takes to get a beer, I am not one of those people.

This year (2017) opened with a fairly ale-heavy Karl Strauss beer lineup. With Mosaic Session IPA joining Hoppyalis and Pintail Pale on the menu, beer connoisseurs are going to be compelled to make multiple trips through this line. Tips for how to maximize enjoyment of incredible Disney beer, without jeopardizing your family's Disney vacation are discussed in our "Disneyland Drinking Gymnastics" chapter. For now, appreciate how the Karl Strauss Beer Truck is moored in the geographic center of the park. Don't make your party stand around while you negotiate your way around the alcohol policy. You will likely pass through this area multiple times during the day.

## *What's to Drink (all 16oz draft)*

- Pintail Pale Ale
- Aurora Hoppyalis IPA

- Mosaic Session IPA
- Follow the Sun Kolsch
- Red Trolley Ale
- Seasonal Beer

# Paradise Garden Grill

*Paradise Pier*
*Serves: Beer, Lunch, Dinner*

Switching between Mediterranean, Mexican, and various cultural cuisines, Paradise Garden is the most novel dining venue this side of Blue Bayou. The menu is categorically good for you, regardless of its current and particular bent. While featuring Mexican cuisine, the rare and glorious Negra Modelo was the beer of the day. Briefly commemorating the Lunar New Year, Korean-style Max Beer was available.

You're probably not going to come this far into the park just to get a beer from Paradise Garden. In conjunction with live entertainment, a beautiful sprawling patio, and some really good and interesting food, you certainly shouldn't avoid the area. Plus, Bayside Brew is right across the walkway. So, you can get your interesting lunch and be assured of excellent beer all year long.

If the Golden Zephyr, Jumpin' Jellyfish, and Silly Symphony Swings attractions do not appeal to you, you have a golden opportunity to secure yourself a drink while your family squanders its own park time. Golden Zephyr looks dull as dishwater from the ground, yet it's deceptively entertaining from the inside. It may have to do with the open doors and the sensation of falling into the lagoon, though I wouldn't fault anyone who opts for an IPA instead.

I've mentioned it several times, but, in the interest of family harmony, you need to be aware of leaving your people on rides with open lines of sight. If you can see your kids, friends, and loved ones on a ride, they can see you getting beer. I don't want you to lie to or abandon your family, no matter how thoroughly I have described methods for doing so. What I really don't want is for anyone to get caught. This ruins everyone's day, quite unnecessarily. So, don't get sloppy.

### What's to Drink (all 16oz draft)

- Negra Modelo
- Max Beer
- Blue Moon
- Red Sangria

# Rita's Baja Blenders

*Pacific Wharf*
*Serves: Margaritas, and what else could you ever need?*

In Epcot, at Walt Disney World, you can get a glass of brightly colored nectar called the Grand Marnier Orange Slush. Consisting mainly of delightful, sugary orange liqueur, if you've had one, you love it. You have since learned, to your frustration, you are powerless to properly re-create it at home.

A Disneyland counterpart may be found at Rita's on the wharf. The discriminating know to spring for the Grand Margarita, which includes a delicious splash of Grand Marnier. It's not quite as compelling as the Epcot cocktail, for which guests will B-line to the farthest reaches of the World Showcase. If the line for the Karl Strauss truck proves prohibitive, a frozen glass of alcoholic candy is an attractive alternative.

If you don't like margaritas, I don't know what to tell you. Well, I mean, I do. There are plenty of other offerings, even within the wharf itself. What I truly mean is I don't understand you. If tequila is that with which you take issue, you needn't worry. Rita's 'ritas do contain the oft-troublesome spirit, though the Grand Marnier masks it rather effectively. It doesn't dampen the effect, and these are quite sweet, so, please watch your intake.

### What's to Drink

- Rita's Margarita
- Rita's Grand Margarita

# Schmoozies

*Hollywood Land*
*Serves: Smoothies; that's it*

Presently, this walk-up window does not serve alcohol. Every time I pass by here and see no line, and see that Mango Madness still does not come with rum in it, I cannot but marvel at the lost opportunity.

# Smokejumpers Grill

*Grizzly Peak*
*Serves: Beer, Sangria, Lunch, Dinner*

Properly committed Disney drinkers are well familiar with Smokejumpers; formerly Taste Pilot's Grill. Until Carthay Circle opened, this was the closest place to the front gate to go for a drink. Arguably, Award Wieners is just as close, but they only have the one beer, with no place to sit, except for the curb right in front of a bathroom.

If you can walk into a Disney park, go right up to the hotdog window, and order a beer, you are a marvel. In Smokejumpers, guests can at least pretend to be over there gathering Soarin' FASTPASSes, and just happen to also be getting a beer.

When making your way through, into, or out of Disney California Adventure, keep Smokejumpers in mind for quick beverage procurement. There can be a line, as they have a number of attractive food items, but there are always a number of registers going. This is not always the case at Award Wieners.

## What's to Drink (all 16oz draft)

- Karl Strauss Handcrafted Beer
- Red Sangria
- Budweiser, Bud Light

***Disney Drinking Tip.*** On the menu at Smokejumpers, they indicate they sell "Karl Strauss Handcrafted Beer." This is deliberate. The selection often changes. It would be a misuse of Disney resources to repaint the signs every time. It behooves guests to check the taps behind the counter before settling on a choice. I once almost committed a tragic Disney drinking blunder. Smokejumpers served Karl Strauss Red Trolley for as long as I can remember. It's a superb brew in its category, though is not on my personal short list. Once, while ordering a sandwich, presuming the status quo, I nearly went without a beer. Then I happened to spot a Tower 10 handle on one of the taps. You can imagine my relief, and, yes, I ordered one.

# Sonoma Terrace

*Pacific Wharf*
*Serves: Beer (12oz), Wine, Quick Bites*

The often overlooked step sibling of the Pacific-Wharf-terrace triumvirate, Sonoma's menu, service, and setting are similarly exquisite. It does not possess the intimacy of Alfresco, or Mendocino's unmatched vantage point, and maintains rather unpredictable hours of operation, and is thus markedly less popular. It is still a beautiful and convenient alternative, and an incredible patio upon which to relax.

Were I a less patient man, Sonoma's vast plot of underutilized real estate is where I would direct all of the families monopolizing Mendocino's limited, enviable tables. I get that many beleaguered parents are just thankful when they can find a place to sit. But, since your kids likely don't care about people watching, you all might be just as happy on Sonoma's slightly less-exposed patio. Then, perhaps, I won't be as regularly disappointed to find the best table in the resort beset by hordes without the proper appreciation for it.

## What's to Drink

- Wine by the glass
- Saint-Hilare, French Sparkling
- Karl Strauss Tower 10 IPA (12oz bottle)
- Anaheim 1888 (12oz bottle)
- Ballast Point Sculpin IPA (12oz bottle)
- Napa Smith Hopageddon (12oz bottle)
- Bud Light (12oz bottle)
- Iron Fist Velvet Glove Imperial Stout (12oz bottle)

# Studio Specialties

*Hollywood Land*
*Serves: Beer, Specialty Drinks, Quick Bites*

Less predictable than the former Luigi's Flying Tires attraction, it is doubtful many guests even know this obscure quick-service counter by name. Sequestered behind Monsters, Inc., Studio Specialties isn't on the map or website, doesn't have a sign you can read, and is almost never open. If you happen to be over there while they're serving, it's a sweet spot to get a drink.

The venue is right next to a kids ride, between two theaters featuring kid-focused entertainment, so I'm not recommending you hang out here and drink. But, it's also in a corner of a less well-traveled section of the park, and, since the cessation of the nightly Mad Tea Party, there is never a line. Plus, they serve margaritas and Stone IPA (subject to change, see unpredictable).

I try never to miss a chance to enjoy Monsters, Inc., the Muppets, or Tower of Terror. With this section of the park now in such a dramatic state of flux, there is no telling what you are going to be able to do in Hollywood Land, or perhaps why you are even over here.

If your party is angling into Sunset Showcase Theater, for whatever gratuitous film preview happens to be back-burnering my beloved Muppets at the time, do yourself, me, and the memory of Jim Henson a favor. If Studio Specialties is open, excuse yourself and head for it.

When your people go on Monsters, Inc., and you decide to get a drink instead, remember, the line winds right past the Studio Specialties counter. When you turn around, with your two drinks, to face the people you just told you were going to sit down for a minute, try not to be taken off guard. The person to whom you attempt to push the "I got one of these for you" lie will be less likely to believe you if you look and act like the guilty liar you are.

## What's to Drink (all 16oz draft)

- Hangar 24 Orange Wheat
- Stone IPA

- Mike's Hard Cranberry Lemonade
- Margarita with Glow Cube
- Rum Island Ice Tea

# Wine Country Trattoria

*Pacific Wharf*
*Serves: Beer, Wine, Cocktails, Lunch, Dinner, Specialty Drinks Menu*

The beating heart of the Golden Vine Winery, this elegant table-service restaurant is the type of place you come when celebrating something noteworthy. Food, service, and setting so spectacular, make sure you don't drink so much you detract from any of it. If you time your meal right, you can sort of see the World of Color from your table.

Control yourself. Still, if you are going to eat here at all, go all the way. Have wine. Have dessert, and get a Godiva Chocolate Martini. Don't share any with your kids. If they complain, wave one hand in a circle to encompass the entire surrounding area, and say, "Tell me again what we did today."

The scant review is hardly worthy of this exquisite restaurant, and its enviable patio. It's just not someplace I would direct anyone looking for a suitable drinking spot. This isn't one. It's a glorious place for dinner, and, okay, wine, with a setting rivaled only by the service.

## *Featured Cocktails*

### Godiva Chocolate Martini
*Godiva Chocolate Liqueur, Stoli Vanil Vodka, White Crème de Cacao, and Frangelico*

### Banana Spiced Rum Martini
*Captain Morgan Original Spiced Rum, Bols Crème de Banana, and RumChata Cream Liqueur*

## *Featured Brews (all 16oz draft)*

- Karl Strauss Tower 10 IPA
- Bear Republic Racer 5 IPA
- Sierra Nevada Pale Ale

# CHAPTER TWO

# Drinking at Disneyland Park

Despite its elusive and ultra-exclusive nature, we are compelled to highlight Club 33, Disney's fabled, member's-only speakeasy. Walt Disney's own former private dining room, Club 33 is even more amazing than you might imagine. If you are a member, we mortals are incurably jealous. If you know a member who can and will get you in, we want to use you to get to know them. If you have even a chance to peek beyond the resolutely closed green door, do so at your earliest opportunity, and consider yourself blessed.

Club 33 offers a full bar. The wine and liquor selection is as inspired as the theme, locale, sentiment, and decor. Not sure about the beer selection. I had wine, and a cocktail. Each was as exquisite as the meal, service, and privileged view.

I was fortunate enough to have dinner at Club 33, once. A couple of dear friends, we'll call them Robert and John, arranged for me, and the woman who would become my wife, to celebrate my 40th birthday there. It was one of those inconceivable bucket list items that's so unlikely, it doesn't belong on the list. I will never be able to properly thank or repay them.

As for a place to eat, get a drink, or even wash your hands, Club 33 has no peer. Just stepping across the threshold puts you in rare company. If you can contain your excitement at a level that allows you to absorb and appreciate the splendor and spectacle of its hallowed halls, then you are a less impulsive individual than I. All of my pictures came out blurry. The extra mints I took melted in my coat. I was reprimanded, rightly, for trying to open the French doors next to our table.

Still, every memory I have of the experience is a degree of wonderful with which only my wedding competes. I don't know how it would be possible, but I've got a mind to get back there someday (hint, hint).

As I say, there is a bar, but I don't think you're supposed to hang out there, or try to directly order a drink from it. At least, I didn't see anyone else doing that, and I wasn't going to be the only one. I could barely breathe for fear of doing something else improper (see French doors). It was all so incredible, yet unreal. I was worried if I even turned the wrong way, I would wake up somewhere else entirely, having dreamed up the entire experience.

Club 33 is the only place to get a drink within the confines of Disneyland, and that's just fine. I would love to drink rum on Pirates of the Caribbean or a beer on a bench on Main Street, but I am okay with not doing that, since it means far fewer drunks inside the park, potentially tainting everyone's childhood memories.

But we can imagine what it would be like if you *could* drink here...

# What-If Disneyland Drinking

I don't want Disneyland to serve alcohol. Having grown up with such wholesome impressions of the Happiest Place on Earth, I am just fine with no one spilling beer on me in line for Big Thunder Mountain. I am equally fine without groups of millennials walking past my family in Fantasyland swearing through a whiskey-addled haze. I am content knowing the sticky puddle on the floorboard of my Autopia vehicle is melted popsicle, not Chardonnay, or something much worse.

True, alcohol is freely available all over the resort, even right outside Disneyland's main gate. And drunk people can still get in. But, most dubious drink-related behavior seems to stay beyond the berm. Knowing they can't get a drink in Toontown helps steer the dedicated drinkers to less child-concentrated pastures. This is surely by Disney design, and is how I prefer it.

If Disneyland ever did sell booze, there are several dream locations for purchasing and relishing an adult refreshment.

I don't ever want to see it happen within my pristine child-hood playground, though I admit if it was available in any of the following spots, I'd be there in line with the rest of you:

## Disneyland Railroad, Main Street Station

Main Street Station is the first attraction you approach as you enter the park. It would draw adults by the trainload, literally, if it had a bar in it. Train travel is a delightful way to move around and see Disneyland. At peak times, it's the only sane way to get through the colossal Adventureland pinch point. Imagine relaxing on the rails with a Hendrick's and tonic, and a cup holder.

Currently, Disney permits guests to board and exit trains at the station of their own choosing. If guests could also drink on the train, there would likely need to be some adjustments to this policy. All the people I consider good friends would happily ride around and around the park until beverage service cut off. You would not want to be in any station when the last-call announcement is made. There would be a nightly stampede, and you wouldn't want anyone you care about to be between it and the bar.

Along with bars, Disney would probably need to incorporate restrooms at the train stations...and pretzel vendors. A dangerous version of the Drinking Around the World game would likely spring up. Again, hope it never happens, but picture the spectacle of people attempting to finish a round of drinks between Main Street and Adventureland Station, then again between Tomorrowland and Main Street. The Disneyland Railroad would begin to resemble some of the more dubious metro transit systems, complete with unconscious bodies and an olfactory presence you would rather not think about, or take with you in your hair and clothes.

## Peter Pan's Flight

Despite sentimental support for Disneyland's park-wide alcohol ban, they should absolutely serve drinks here. Unless you sprint directly to Peter Pan at the rope drop, you will not get on this ride without a 45-minute wait. In the summer it's an hour, or more. Peter Pan's popularity is understandable. The detail, concept, and story combine for easily the best Fantasyland attraction. No disrespect for Alice in Wonderland, but flying pirate ship tops self-righteous caterpillar ten times out of ten.

If you have kids, they want to go on Peter Pan every time you visit. If you don't have kids, but are still sentimental, you want to ride it every couple of years. Either way, everyone eventually has to endure this glacier of a line. Even when the park doesn't seem that busy, this ride is. It's just such a slow loader, and they only average about 2.1 bodies per flying boat.

Most people boarding this ride appear to be doing so for the first time. Given the sheer numbers churning through the queue on a yearly basis, this cannot possibly be true. Yet, when it comes time to board, people approach the boat with a trepidation that makes the terribly slow line easier to comprehend. It's like people think the boat is either going to take off without them, or fall out of the sky. It's not. Just so you know. Do the people behind you a favor. GET IN THE BOAT!

There's nothing Disney can do to speed up the ride without changing it, and they don't dare do that. This is a true classic. Over the years they have tinkered with the line; adding switchbacks and one of those helpful "From This Point, You Are Going to Miss Lunch and the Parade" notices. But, space and semantics prevent any helpful refurbishment. It would take an entire additional track to make a meaningful difference. Disney would never do this, but I wonder how disruptive it would be to remove Pinocchio or Snow White's Scary Adventures, and just have two Peter Pan attractions. I like all the Fantasyland dark rides, but I wouldn't weep for long about the loss of one of those two, if it means doubling my chances of getting on Peter Pan.

At Walt Disney World's Magic Kingdom, the Peter Pan line winds through a delightful and distracting interior mockup of the Darling children's home. Climate control and interactive elements help significantly mitigate the excessive wait. The Florida Peter Pan also has a FastPass line, which all but cancels out the positive adjustments to the standby queue. If Disneyland can employ some of the interaction, without the FastPass, it might be worthwhile. They might have to shut down one of their primary attractions for a while to achieve it. Likely why they haven't done so yet.

The solution then: cocktails! The new problem: as with Space Mountain, Haunted Mansion, or even the Tiki Room; every line you attempt to improve by inserting alcohol, you will instantly worsen the wait time. Seems counterproductive, right?

The thing for guests and Imagineers to work out is how much more time in line are people willing to tolerate for Bloody Mary access. It won't be the same for everyone, but I bet Disney can focus-group a generally suitable algorithm. Then, say they determine that for every one adult beverage, guests demonstrate they are willing to endure fifteen more minutes in line.

With that information, Disney can institute a floating beverage-station system. They then put a rollaway bar at the head of the queue, and another one every fifteen minutes up the line until you reach the front. You would still have to pay for drinks, of course. No one would be required to make a purchase at every, or even any, station, and if you didn't want drinks, you could skip past the people in front of you who do. Those who want to reach the front completely content, according to the research, will take full advantage of the scientifically orchestrated refreshment network.

So, yeah, I'm no more serious about this than any other Disneyland interior drinking scheme. I shudder to think of this steady stream of adults, having just had two, three, four, perhaps more cocktails, flowing out into Fantasyland. Imagine the havoc they will wreak when they discover the other attractions aren't participating in the beverage-rationing experiment. The poor churro vendor who gets caught in their rage wave wouldn't stand a chance.

## Blue Bayou

The poor man's Club 33, Blue Bayou would be an amazing place to enjoy an adult beverage. Imagine sharing a bottle of wine at dinner in this already romantic Southern nightscape. If the Monte Cristo Sandwich does not call out for the accompaniment of a Bourbon and Coke, I don't know what does. What better way to stave off fried-cheesy-sandwich lethargy than with caffeine and firewater?

As with many Disneyland drinking fantasies, this one inherently confounds itself. It's already fairly difficult to get a table at Blue Bayou. It is even hard to walk past the restaurant at lunchtime. To help accommodate more guests, the dining room is now so packed with tables that people sitting on either side of you have to help you order. Servers essentially crowd surf to and from the kitchen. Throw in cocktail servers and guests' commensurate unwillingness to leave, and it might well be easier to get into Club 33 upstairs.

## The Many Adventures of Winnie the Pooh

There is something about this ride that I just do not understand. I adore the works of A. A. Milne; have since I was a toddler. I am also familiar with the Heffalumps and Woozles reference. What I don't grasp is why Heffalumps and Woozles dominate an entire Disneyland attraction.

They were the basis of a charming song and scene in the Winnie the Pooh movie, and passing references in a couple of the books. If this ride is your primary exposure to the Winnie the Pooh story, you would presume Milne and a few Disney Imagineers suffered substance abuse issues. You would be afraid to let your kids read the books. I am nervous to take mine on this ride, or even ride it myself.

I find something delivered in a shot glass helps clear up confusion. Rather, in my experience, shots help to mollify that which is otherwise baffling. It's not that I gain clarity, more that I care less, and then can embrace the bizarre in a manner that renders it less frustrating. Of course, what straight alcohol is likely to do in this situation is render the psychedelic dark ride into something even more terrifying.

Here, then, we see the inherent contradiction of drinking inside Disneyland itself. The best way to comprehend this particular children's attraction is to blunt your consciousness and judgment. Correspondingly, the worst way to approach anything that is designed to simultaneously attract and distress children (see Toontown) is with your faculties blunted.

Another pressing issue: if you come out of the Winnie the Pooh ride under the influence, you may forget your aversion to Splash Mountain, right next door. It's not that Splash Mountain isn't positively charming and a delightful thrill ride. Because it is. The problem is you always seem to get disproportionately soaked, at least way more than anyone else in your log.

## Space Mountain Queue

You ever come up to Space Mountain to find a 45-minute standby line? All the time, right? Do you get in it anyway? This was a far more common occurrence before FastPass. Clearly, there are still enough people willing to suffer such inconvenience, or the line wouldn't so frequently be that long.

You ever stand out on that top deck, before the line winds into the building, and think, "What have I done?" Again, every time, huh? I personally haven't ridden Space Mountain standby in years, except during those off-peak times when the line doesn't extend out that far. And I will never do it in direct sunlight. Can't see why anyone does. As I skirt the unwary and unfortunate, on my way through the FASTPASS entrance, especially during the day, what I imagine I would be thinking is, "Where is that waitress?"

With cocktail service, or even just a bar posted on the ramp where the line starts, Space Mountain wouldn't need FAST-PASS. The resultant standby wait wouldn't be nearly as bad if you weren't constantly giving way to FASTPASSers. With a beverage in your hand, it wouldn't matter as much, anyway.

Margaritas would save lives on that interminable stint on the patio in direct sunlight. Even if Disney isn't willing to do that (and, remember, we don't really want them to), it's surprising they don't have cast members up there selling snow cones, or something similar. Disney certainly isn't shy about exploitative yet wonderful money making endeavors (see *Frozen*). Selling candy-flavored ice to a sweltering, captive audience seems like a no-brainer.

## Frontierland Shootin' Exposition

When you go to the shooting gallery, with a friend or loved one, you wager on it, right? Well, the only thing better than gallery shooting and gambling is gallery shooting, gambling, and drinking. Like bowling and fishing, my target shooting actually improves with a little booze in me.

When shootin' under the influence, the wagon train targets way in the back, tracking across the desert horizon, are a waste of your shots, time, and tokens. They're hard to hit while sober, and would be so even if they weren't moving. If you have bet anything substantial, or if you are simply, desperately trying to impress someone, stick to the gravestones and similar foreground targets. They may not be impressive, but neither is missing every shot. When a Disney shooting gallery rifle fires, and is not immediately followed by the sounds of piano music, crows, dynamite, or dancing cactus, people on Tom Sawyer Island can hear your echoing shame. Your friends or prospective love interest will never say it, but that will be the moment they stopped respecting you.

It would be a blast to have, and be able to bet, drinks here. However, between the language, empty bottles, and underworld element, the shootin' gallery would quickly become really uncomfortable and inappropriate for kids. Also, a bunch of us would just ignore the targets altogether, to see how far we can shoot into the park. It would be hilarious to start lighting up unwitting guests on the *Mark Twain* riverboat. It might even take years, and pockets full of tokens, before the drinkin', freelancin' shooters figure out the guns emit infrared, not visible light. Even with this knowledge, a bunch of us would still do it.

## Autopia

This is a terrible idea, in a section that is full of them. There is no part of me that believes alcohol and automobiles ought to be combined, especially within a haven of highly influenced children. But, just hear me out...

Autopia has one of those lines that seems to drag. Maybe it's something in the water, but Nemo, the monorail, Tomorrowland railroad station, many attractions in this area all load significant groups of guests into their cars, trains, and submarines, at reasonable intervals, yet the queues seem to move backwards. The sensation would be much more pleasurable, and easier to ignore, with beer in the equation. Don't believe me? Have you ever sat through an entire baseball game, in person, without drinking?

Disney turned the Autopia waiting area into a sort of grand-stand about a decade ago, but didn't do much to alleviate the time in line. Not sure if it is an intentional byproduct, but we now spend a good deal more time in the sun. No Disneyland attraction will ever rival Walt Disney World for unpleasant exposure to the elements. But, when the West Coast Autopia wait time exceeds twenty minutes, which is almost always, along with Dumbo, this is arguably the worst line in the park. (For the record, the worst line in the resort is over at Toy Story Midway Mania! The Radiator Springs standby queue is typi-cally the longest, but if you get in that, you have only your-self to blame. What makes Toy Story Mania so frustrating is partly how long it is, but also how it's so confoundingly slow. The new FASTPASS arrangement will help those who get them. The standby line is going to petrify.)

So, to make the Autopia experience less excruciating, and keep it family friendly, divide the queue between drinkers and designated drivers. This, naturally, solves every issue. Those given to boredom may opt to have a cocktail in line, they just have to forgo the pleasure of operating the Autopia vehicle. Anyone who wants to drive may do so, provided they commit to remaining sober. At the head of the queue, guests from both lines are matched up, ensuring two riders per car. With no more single drivers the line would move almost twice as fast. For the drinking line, it would feel even faster.

Am I proposing we risk pairing up children with drunken strangers in this scenario? Well, not now. Not when you put it that way. It would have a bit of a scared-straight element, from which the children might benefit. Yet, I recall an airplane ride where I unwittingly became the captive audience of a man well past the legal limit. Any life lesson a child is going to learn about substance abuse could well be lost in the fact they're trapped in a motor vehicle with a completely unpredictable, unknown adult with demonstrated impatience issues.

## Essentially Anywhere in New Orleans Square

Have you been to New Orleans, the one in Louisiana, as a drinking-age adult? Do you wish you could do the whole thing over again, with a little less shame and binge drinking?

NOLA is one of those places that force feeds one's compulsions. Worse, it grabs them by the throat, throws them in a cage, pokes them with a stick, then sets them loose on a network of city streets with cheap drinks and bars that never close.

Disney's version is so much more wholesome. They should almost call it something else. It would be delightful to re-create certain elements of a New Orleans vacation at Disneyland, where it's safe, clean, and there's almost no chance you're going to pay for something you couldn't later justify to a sober version of yourself.

No, Disneyland should not import the unbridled emotion, smell, or 4-for-1 Happy Hour, but wouldn't it be wonderful to have a real mint julep while listening to the jazz band on the patio of the French Market Restaurant? The best part would be remembering just exactly how you got the beads around your neck, and not being the least bit worried about it.

## Buzz Lightyear Astro Blasters

The Buzz Lightyear line isn't typically that bad. Cocktail service for a smoothly flowing queue and attraction that requires thorough guest participation seems misplaced. I suggest it only because of a personal, emotionally scarring incident I experienced on this ride some years ago. I'm still not over it.

I made a friendly Buzz Lightyear wager with a lovely woman I was dating, over who would score more points. At the time I was unaware certain targets were worth substantially more points than certain other targets. She knew. She also knew I didn't know, and she didn't tell me about it. She beat me as if I were blindfolded.

Every time I even walk near Tomorrowland, much less within sight of Buzz Lightyear, I feel like I want to cry. I also want a drink. Something exceedingly strong that numbs pain, that silences screaming, that dulls memories of the churro I had to buy, to pay off the bet that was lost as soon as it was made.

No, I don't think there should be alcohol inside Disneyland. There are many reasons, not the least of which is because I don't want to wind up on my knees in front of Buzz, with a fistful of churros, empty whiskey bottle in the other hand, shouting "Whyyy?" into the uncaring infinite distance.

### Every Meet-and-Greet Character Experience

Alcohol does not have a direct negative effect on children, unless of course a kid gets his hands on a bottle of something. The issue that concerns me is what alcohol often does to supposed grownups. It causes un-adult behavior, to which children should not be subjected, especially at Disneyland.

A meet-and-greet, then, is the last place you should drink, which is a shame, because it's exactly where you need to (see, also, Toontown). The contradiction is profound. On one hand we've got droves of little angels, all charged up and enamored over meeting their real-life heroes in person. If we could just embrace that, and let the beauty of it fill us up, the whole experience could be all-ages wonderful.

Instead, what do the adults do? We focus on the line, and the heat, the not being on the Matterhorn, and the noise. Then, the four year old behind you keeps pushing past you, stepping on your foot, and generally not at all keeping his proper place in line. Then we start calculating how much each minute in line is costing us, as it relates to the price of admission, and how there's no way you're going to make your Star Tours FASTPASS window.

Mixing adult beverages into this already precarious recipe could well blow up the kitchen. Instead of a full bar, then, maybe a cast member could walk the line with trays of champagne and jello shooters?

### Park Bench on Main Street

Every visit to Disneyland ought to include at least a couple minutes sitting on one of those green benches around the Hub, at the castle end of Main Street. The compulsion to spend an entire Disney day hustling from attraction, to attraction, to lunch, to attraction, to restroom, without a moment's peace, is nigh undeniable. There is so much to do, and see, and ride, and eat, if you slow down for even a moment, you feel you must surely be missing something.

Just once, though, even if you have to force yourself, take a seat somewhere. Stop for a moment. Look up at the sky. Take in the landscape. Watch other people furiously hustle by, the way you used to. Give yourself a minute. Then you may get up and run to the next pressing need on your list.

Once you enjoy Disneyland through the eyes and placid brain of the intentionally pensive, you will begin to crave it. The people watching at a Disney park is rivaled only by that of other Disney parks. Now, imagine the experience with a frozen margarita in your hands, and system. Absolute paradise.

Yes, you can absolutely replicate the experience across the esplanade at Disney California Adventure. And so you should. Still, there would be something that much more magical sipping on an IPA, within the shadows and influence of Sleeping Beauty Castle.

## *"it's a small world"*

It has long been chic to say you don't like "it's a small world." Mysteriously, the aquatic, hypnotic singalong remains immensely well visited. With a few minor additions, it could be the most popular ride in the park—namely, a portable bar at the head of the line, and permission to bring drinks with you into the little boats.

Parents would be dragging their little ones onto this ride. You would also see an entirely different composition of guests in line. Couples with brightly colored plastic cups would be overheard discussing how they've always liked the little song. Twenty somethings would cash in favors to get their younger siblings to ride with them, for the sake of appearances. Middle-age adults, without kids, will still probably wonder if it's creepy for them to ride, yet, content with a couple Manhattans in tow, would do it anyway.

If anything can salvage the last five minutes of this ride, it's a frosty beverage. I'm not referring to the final scene where kids from every culture come together for one last rousing rendition of everyone's favorite melody. Rather, I mean the home stretch where you come out of the building, into the blistering sunshine. No matter the weather when your ride starts, while you are in the building, the sun invariably comes out and the local temperature jumps by twenty degrees. For equally inexplicable reasons, this is where the slow, but smoothly moving vessels all come to a resolute halt. I understand that the dock is up ahead, and the wait comes from the exiting and re-boarding process. Strangely, everywhere else, along the entire route, the boats remains in motion. Except here. And always, as mentioned, in direct sunlight.

If there was a vending machine next to the big, whimsical "adios" banner at the end, and it sold hundred-dollar Mojitos, I would hawk my annual pass for one, every time.

## Mickey's Toontown

The absence of alcohol, which I still support, has much to do with how rarely I venture into Toontown. I love children. I share a home and life with a couple of them. They are wonderful. They love Disneyland. My wife and I have managed to exert a subtle but stern influence on them over the years, whereby they aren't interested in Toontown either. We are a happier, more functional family because of it.

Toontown has its place for families who profess to enjoy such stimulation. Who am I to judge? Some people like fighting over bacon-wrapped ice cream at Hometown Buffet. I celebrate our diversity. For me to be comfortable in the high-energy flytrap that lurks out behind Fantasyland, however, would require a large glass with vodka in it.

The area itself is as charming and clever as anything else Disney designers put their hands to. When I've managed to explore it on rare, lightly trafficked occasions, i.e., during a runDisney half marathon before the park opens, I have enjoyed it thoroughly. Fill it with the level of running, screaming, infantile panic that more commonly infests its every acre, and I start rousting cast members for muscle relaxers.

So, yeah, Toontown is ripe for beverage service. But, like ground zero with a happy hour, it won't fix what's wrong. Not really. We can't be trusted to consume liquor in the same square mile where everyone under a certain age believes the talking animals are real.

## Enchanted Tiki Room

Can you imagine anything more refreshing and fulfilling than a Dole Whip Float with booze in it? Floridians have been savoring them for decades, but Walt Disney World doesn't allow alcohol in the Magic Kingdom, either. The Disneyland Hotel now serves them if you happen to know how to locate the Coffee House. You'll never get one of those into the park, though.

Imagine sitting in the sun-dappled Adventureland courtyard, taking in water features and talking Tiki gods, with a rum-soaked cup of pineapple soft-serve splendor. Similar to "it's a small world," the Tiki Room would witness a serious uptick in popularity. Sure, many would simply make their way out through the turnstile once they've secured a beverage, but others, like myself, who like to sit a while and savor, would become Tiki, Tiki, Tiki, Tiki, Tiki Room regulars.

Here is another situation where reality defies the fantasy. Unless you have tried to get a Dole Whip from Disneyland in a driving rainstorm, there is always a line; even at night. If our particular Tiki Juice Bar sold rum, the wait for even a napkin would be prohibitive. Nice to consider, though.

## *The Golden Horseshoe*

Good food. A clean, comfortable table inside a charmingly appointed concert hall. Exceptionally clever live entertainment. What more could you ask for? Well, if you've followed this guide at all, you know what's missing: some good, old-fashioned hooch.

Like in any worthwhile comedy club, the Golden Horseshoe Revue would kill with a two-drink minimum. On its own, the show is terrific. Imagine it with a room full of the more easily influenced and impressionable. Face it, drinkers, that's undeniably what we are, and those are a couple of our better traits.

In keeping with Frontierland theming, they could serve warm beer and grain alcohol. Guests could sidle up to the bar, throw down a silver dollar, and say, "whiskey," nonspecifically. A kind, but completely unappreciated barkeep will appear instantly, despite a blatantly full bar, and leave an entire bottle. You pull the cork out—the bottle would have a cork rather than a cap—with your teeth, and drink straight whiskey as if it were tea. There are Westerns where the characters throw down their drink in one go, while others order entire rounds that go wholly neglected. You are free to pursue either, based upon your tolerance and your appreciation for the cinematic arts.

Considering the area, Rancho del Zocalo Restaurante seems like it would be another primo venue for adult refreshment. Alas, it is not. It isn't that a Negra Modelo wouldn't be wonderful with your meal, on the quaint patio beneath the spires of Big Thunder Mountain. Nay, human nature is the problem. What is to stop a guest from drinking several cervezas, eating an entire Red Chile Enchilada Platter, then going directly onto Big Thunder Mountain Railroad? Nothing. So, that's exactly what would happen. And it is yet another of the many reasons Disneyland does not, and should not, serve us alcohol.

## *Mark Twain* Riverboat/Sailing Ship *Columbia*

As with the Disneyland Railroad, described above, imagine the pleasure of sitting topside on a Rivers of America watercraft, whiling away an afternoon with your drink-of-choice coursing through your system. Were this even an option, more people would dash over here at rope drop than to Space Mountain, Peter Pan, and the Matterhorn combined. It would require fire alarms to get people off those boats.

The *Mark Twain* is an ideal way to steal a few minutes of slow-down during an all-out Disneyland visit. It's even better when you can get one of the few seats on the foredeck. With a few more places to sit, and a sloe gin cocktail, I could see this becoming my favorite attraction. That is, unless the *Columbia* served drinks, too. There would be some fairly spectacular impromptu Fantasmic reenactments by enthusiastic rum-swilling guests. I can't promise I wouldn't join the pirate rebellion, and participate in a not-entirely-peaceful takeover of Tom Sawyer Island.

Until Star Wars Land is complete, we need only speculate how wonderful such developments might be. I still don't want booze inside Disneyland, but as *Mark Twain* and *Columbia* sit in dry dock, I can't help hoping, when they return, Disney will put my nightly dinner cruise idea into practice.

## *Esplanade Ticket Booths*

Not located inside Disneyland, specifically, but, oh, what a difference it would make starting off a Disney day if you could get a glass of anything with booze in it in those awful lines. A committed annual passholder, I rarely have to contend with the twisted agony of the ticket booth plaza. Still, I never fail to empathize with those who do.

You finally make up your mind to travel to Disneyland. Be it with family, friends, or even solo, a significant financial and temporal investment stretches out before you. If I ever let my pass expire, I will procure every ticket I ever need online. The prospect of standing in a lengthy line, waiting to drop a bundle of money, before I even get near the front gate and all the lines and expenses inside, is horrifying.

The cast members who work the ticket windows are as friendly, capable, and efficient as any in the resort, but the nature of many ticket purchases creates and sustains the slowly moving queue. I want nothing to do with it.

A bar at the head of each line would greatly salvage the experience, and do wonders for those suffering through it. Disney is certainly not in the habit of bilking its guests, but an adult beverage or two might even help sell a few extra annual passes. If this ever happens, I can see my friends holding it against me. Being a couple grand down before you even get into the park can be unnerving, but everyone captains their own ship.

# CHAPTER THREE

# Drinking at the Disneyland Resort Hotels

All guests of the Disneyland Resort are welcome to tour and take advantage of many of the hotel property amenities. You can't use the pool unless you're staying at a particular property, and we've yet to successfully sway room service to deliver food or drinks to the lobby, but all restaurants are open for your patronage, and everyone has virtual free rein of the grounds. More to our area of concern, every Disneyland Resort bar is open to the age-appropriate public.

You should be aware of a truly perplexing situation at the Disney hotel properties, involving the pricing of light beer. While loathe to recommend light beer at the parks, where California's finest craft brews await the discerning drinker, I fault no one for grabbing a couple Coors Light cans for their hotel room. I am not a huge fan of paying $7 for a can of Coors, but we're a captive audience here. Between the gift shops and hotel eateries, Coors Light is available in about twenty different locations. The price per ounce is different at every one.

Had the issue involved any of the fine Karl Strauss products, I would have bought them all; for the sake of accuracy. I mention it only as it strikes me as interesting how a 16-ounce Coors Light appears to cost less from Disney's Grand Californian gift shop than a 12-ounce Coors Light from the snack bar a hundred feet away. Yeah, I need a hobby. Well, another hobby; besides this one.

# Disneyland Hotel

Staying at the Disneyland Hotel? I commend you on your good fortune and judgment. Every room is amazing. So, in fact, is the entire property. The first thing you need to do is turn on your bed's illuminated headboard and post pictures of it to everyone who you know that's working at that particular moment. (If you are checking in during the day, you can still do it, just shut the curtains first.) If you get a room facing the park, try to be in it when the fireworks go off at 9:25 that night.

If you've simply ventured all the way over to the Disneyland Hotel in search of a drink, wouldn't it be something if they didn't serve alcohol? Not to worry. They do, at several delightful locations. Between Goofy's Kitchen, gift shops, pool service, and a theater-like Tiki bar, the Disneyland Hotel is an amazing all-ages attraction of its own. Now, if they would bring back the old arcade and dancing waters light show....

## *Goofy's Kitchen*

*Serves: Full Bar, Breakfast, Lunch, Dinner, Specialty Drinks Menu*

Yes, you can get alcohol at the character breakfast. We asked. They have a full bar, in fact. It's not a bar to which you can go—retreat, rather—drink, and hide from your family. There is one of those in the Steakhouse 55 Lounge (see below), and it's a fine place to wait for your Goofy table. The lounge bar isn't open during breakfast. Not that people wouldn't take advantage of it. It's more that you shouldn't.

So, Goofy's Kitchen features a service bar. This allows you to accompany your family to the whimsical character breakfast without losing your mind. Honestly, grownups ought to give the event a proper chance. Disneyland Resort Hotel cast members are every bit as professional and capable as their theme park compatriots. You'll feel like you are in the park, and all but the most incredulous child won't know the difference. If your children's joy is not enough to balance out a character meal worth of chaos, that's what Bloody Marys are for.

If you target a specifically child-friendly character-themed restaurant as somewhere to go for a drink, we implore you to practice responsible behavior. There are kids everywhere. They are there to see the huge dog in the chef's hat. For everyone under the legal drinking age, nothing about the experience is made better by you overdoing it on mimosas.

True, the children, giant dogs, and mayhem are why you want a drink so badly in the first place. Still, limit yourself, intentionally. You likely have a long day of roller coasters and giant turkey legs ahead of you. In a few hours, say, on the teacups, your kids won't be the only ones thankful you pulled back on the drinking at breakfast.

## Steakhouse 55

*Serves: Beer, Wine, Full Bar, Breakfast,*
*Dinner, Specialty Drinks Menu*

By the time you get to the Steakhouse 55 lounge, there is commonly a sizable spillover crowd from Goofy's Kitchen occupying most of the space and furniture. When the cast opens up the Steakhouse bar, it's always to a near-mob of expectant, yet blank faces. Exercise patience in everything you do at Disneyland. When conducting business with an already overwrought bartender, please be especially compassionate.

Limited in space, furniture, and menu, Steakhouse 55 is a glorious, if unexpected spot to spend a few minutes, when you can find a seat. The waiting-for-Goofy's-Kitchen contingent can make matters a bit hectic. When you take this for the spectacular people-watching opportunity it is, this lounge reveals itself as a true hidden entertainment gem. With the proper seats at the bar, or an outward-facing table, treat yourself to a game of condemning complete strangers through snap judgments of their parenting skills.

The rules are simple: watch for children, who do not know each other, to take a simultaneous interest in the classic Autopia race car in the foyer. Dubious parenting will manifest itself in several forms. First we have those who will let their kids completely dominate a public point of interest. Next we have the absentee offenders, who will leave their own flesh and blood bawling in a heap, as they covertly enjoy a glass of wine at the table right next to you. Then there are those who refuse to even let their kids take part in the competitive ballet. A toddler who winds up screaming on the simulated brickwork because someone got a longer turn than they did is one matter. The child who is forced to stand idly by, and spectate from a distance as others in their demographic enjoy a private slice of Disneyland before their eyes, is experiencing a form of cruelty. My parents fell into a separate category. They gave me all the love, advice, guidance, and attention I could ever desire, yet I was still the kid who would end up getting hurt, improperly using the escalator.

## Featured Cocktails

### The French 75
*Nolet's Silver Gin, fresh Lemon Juice, Simple Syrup, Sparkling Wine*

### Blood Orange Mimosa
*Zonin Prosecco, Blood Orange Puree*

## Featured Brews (all 16oz draft)

- Karl Strauss Aurora Hoppyalis
- Ballast Point Sculpin IPA

## *Tangaroa Terrace*
*Serves: Beer, Wine, Breakfast, Lunch,*
*Dinner, Open Early (7am–10pm)*

Before the extensive, 21st-century Disneyland Hotel remodel, the property was alive with dancing waters, remote control boats, and one outstanding arcade. The central patio was also home to a delightful open-air bar. I am growing to love Trader Sam's, the new pool, and everything that now occupies this space, though I will probably never get over the loss of the reasonably priced burgers and the room full of video games that I used to be good at.

With the removal of that bar and the opening of Downtown Disney's Earl of Sandwich, I don't take quick meals at the hotel nearly as often. Tangaroa Terrace possesses plenty of Disney charm, atmosphere, and wonderful, smiling service, but Earl of Sandwich is just so much closer to the monorail station.

One hundred times out of a hundred, I would rather have a Kona brew from Trader Sam's over a Tangaroa Heineken. The families and conventioneers who got their first, taking up every Trader Sam's seat, do not care about my preferences.

Trader Sam's extraordinary cast members care. However, they are often overworked, and it's not Disney policy to hurry guests out of their restaurants. Thus, they can do little to get you a table when there isn't one.

Tangaroa Terrace, then, often proves the more convenient option for getting a beer, even if it is a notably lesser beer. If you are on the go, this is absolutely your best bet—that is, if you are headed to your room (you lucky dog), or to the pool, and don't think you can get a good chaise in the server's current rotation.

Trying to take a beer from Tangaroa into Downtown Disney earns you a visit from the White Hats. Since the security bag check moved, they don't even have to chase you down any more. Unwitting offenders literally present themselves for inspection. It's not quite Trader Sam's, but sit for a moment, on the terrace, and finish your beer. If you time it right, from every seat on the Trader Sam's patio you can hear, and from most you can still see, the live entertainment.

## What's to Drink
- Mike Hess Double IPA (12oz can)
- Heineken (16oz bottle)
- Bud Light (16oz bottle)
- Coors Light (12oz bottle)

### *Trader Sam's Enchanted Tiki Bar*
*Serves: Full Bar, Lunch, Dinner, Open Late (1:30am)*

You have to see this place to appreciate it. Bring the family. Take a tour. Witness as enthusiastic cast members spray and yell things at the guests. Now, take your kids back to the park.

Yes, Trader Sam's is authentic Disney-inspired charm and entertainment. It's also a bar. Trader Sam's offers a full food menu, which will tempt you to sit down for lunch. Just know that all your hamburger eating grunions make it difficult for the rest of us to get timely cocktail service.

Trader Sam's serves Bud Light. If you order one, they should shoot you with spray bottles. They won't. That particular indignity is reserved for patrons of more elaborate beverages. What you ought to do, threat of spray bottles notwithstanding, is order a drink you don't recognize, with an enticing name and/ or description. This is absolutely that type of place.

Fire open a menu. If you are not tempted to order a Piranha Pool or Passionate Python, then perhaps you aren't properly Tiki-bar motivated. Drinks with which you are familiar can be procured anywhere. Trader Sam's has a wine list, but where's the adventure? Most Trader Sam's specialty drinks come with a bit of a performance from the cast members, and a fair amount of pyrotechnics. I won't spoil the surprise, but ordering specific cocktails triggers a rainstorm and volcanic eruption. Ordering a Chardonnay gets you a Chardonnay, and my disapproval.

If you absolutely can't handle a complicated mixed drink, craft beer is an acceptable option, provided you order the right beer. We don't mean to be unfair to Bud Light, but a tropical Tiki bar is not the spot for it. Pretty much anywhere outside of a Big Ten tailgate party also isn't ideal, but again, we're not trying to pile on. Several Kona Brewing Company varieties are always available. Any one of these may spark memories of wonderful moments you've spent on a beach somewhere, if not actual flashing lights in the walls and ceiling.

Trader Sam's does not serve a Dole Whip Cocktail. It is the undisputed world's most appropriately themed venue for such, and ought to sell them. It is not an outrageous oversight by the Disney people, however. It isn't even terribly surprising. You've been there. It's crowded. Always. Now throw in one of Disney's most popular tropical treats, with alcohol in it. You already can't get a table inside unless you help open the place. With Dole Whip Rum Cocktails, they'd need a FASTPASS entrance.

## Featured Cocktails

### Uh Oa!
*Light and Dark Rums, Orange, Passion Fruit, Guava, Pineapple, Grapefruit Juices, Falernum, Cinnamon, and fresh Lime Juice (serves 2)*

### Mosquito Mojito
*Strawberry Rum, Organic Agave Nectar, Falernum, Mint, and fresh Lime Juice topped with Soda Water*

## Featured Brews (all 16oz draft)

- Kona Fire Rock Pale Ale
- Karl Strauss Tower 10 IPA

## Neverland Poolside

*Serves: Beer, Wine, Full Bar, Full Menu, Specialty Drinks*

To use the Disneyland Hotel pool, you must be a guest of the Disneyland Hotel. I don't think they even call it the Neverland Pool anymore. It's how I remember it, so I'm going with that. My lasting memories are of a massive lap pool, to the east of what is now the Adventure Tower. As rather an intrusive kid, I weep for anyone who ever tried to swim laps while I was in the pool.

Properly budgeting your time between this incredible hotel property and the rest of the resort will be an issue. When anywhere within shouting distance of a Disney park, it's difficult to justify spending time anywhere else. This Disneyland Hotel, and its multi-pool-and-waterslide complex, is well worth any time you choose to dedicate to it, even at the expense of two parks full of charmingly themed roller coasters.

Even if just making your way from the front desk to your room, take advantage of the pool. Specifically, as it pertains to this book, get yourself a drink by the pool. Delightful Disney cast members will eagerly bring great frothing chalices of colorful, frozen splendor right to your chaise lounge. If you have any difficulty justifying the cost of an exotic poolside cocktail, take a look at the mournful strangers on the other side of the fence wishing they were you.

The role of the poolside server is as difficult as it is under-appreciated. It's not that they are working any harder than, say, the poor hustling bodies over at Trader Sam's. But, at a bar, restaurant, quick-service counter, etc., guests can at least get a glimmer of what is going on. We can sort of see how many other patrons are around, how much help there is, how many tables have food versus how many are waiting to order. Around a pool, guests have very little grasp of, and not much compassion for, what a server is going through. There can be a hundred thirsty sunbathers spread out around a patio, with one person to serve them, and each of those hundred people might have the same unreasonable expectation of rapid, preferential treatment.

Always be kind to cast members, and absolutely exercise patience regarding pool service. You are the one enjoying a lazy day in the sun. The poor kid with the apron and tiny tray is working. They are working for you, and everyone else who gets to hang out by a beautiful swimming pool that day. Receiving pool service is a privilege. This means, fundamentally, you lack the ambition to go up to Trader Sam's and get your own drinks.

In addition to, and greatly exacerbated by, pool-guest oblivion, the system works against the server. Again, unlike a restaurant, almost no one registers who is their particular pool server. Thus, everyone with a nametag who passes within eyesight and earshot is as good as our own personal servant. A guest in need of attention, or ketchup, will tackle a server to get it, regardless of how many Mai Tais or turkey melts that cast member has on their tray.

**Disney Pool Drinking Tip.** It can take even the best, most efficient server a long, long time to make their way around their station. To secure a quick initial beverage, before you even claim a deck chair, locate a server, preferably the one who least looks like they wish they were somewhere else, and try to get ahead of them.

Wait your turn. Politely get their attention if necessary. Respectfully place your order. Offer to pay on delivery, rather than running a tab. This step is vital, because what you are also going to do, then, is ask if you can meet them as they exit the service area and claim your drink. Special concessions seldom make a server's day, but if you remain polite throughout this exchange, and treat the person you are speaking with like an equal and fellow human being, rather than some underling, they might agree. Be the type of customer that is a pleasure to serve, and watch your service improve non-coincidentally.

Unless you already know where the service area is—the place servers retreat to fill orders and steal fleeting moments of sanity—be sure to ask, or pay specific attention where they go as they leave "the floor." Be there, smiling, as they come back and tip copiously. Not only have you saved yourself the inconvenience of waiting for a server to slog their way, twice, around the entire pool, kindness and generosity are the best means of securing preferential future service.

Yes, I have essentially described a method of bribing a cast member, which would seem to go against the general Disney spirit. Their deeply ingrained philosophy is to provide every guest with extra-special treatment. Many cast members are young kids, and, hey, they're all human. Just because they're programmed to provide unconditionally wonderful hospitality does not mean they won't appreciate a little kind consideration in return.

Also, please do not be offended, or even surprised, if this approach fails. Some servers organize their tray to correspond to how the orders were taken, and are thus to be dispensed. The prospect of you coming along and upsetting the balance will not appeal to these cast members. You may just have to wait your turn, or drift up to Trader Sam's on your own.

## *small world Gifts & Sundries*

*Sells: Beer, Wine, Snacks,  Open Early (7am)*

Desperate for a beer? Don't feel like waiting for a server? First, calm down. Try to remember where you are. There are kids everywhere, including all throughout the hotels. Now then, this particular gift shop features a small drinks cooler. Beer and wine may be purchased for a predictable premium, and they'd rather you didn't stand there and drink in the store. Don't ask me how I know that.

If you have a room, what you purchase here is meant to be enjoyed there. Adults may, within Disney rules, consume alcohol on the hotel grounds. Do not try to take beer from the Disneyland Hotel into Downtown Disney District. You can guess how I know about this.

### What's to Drink

- Red, White, Blush Wine by the bottle
- Blue Moon (12oz bottle)
- Corona (12oz bottle)
- Heineken (12oz bottle)
- Bud Light (16oz bottle)
- Coors Light (12oz bottle)

Here continues the great light-beer mystery. In this gift shop, Coors Light costs more than a larger Bud Light. Just up the ramp at Tangaroa Terrace (see complete review, above), Coors Light costs less, for the same size can. Any understanding I developed on the matter, as to why prices are disparate between restaurants and gift shops, is blown up by the Heineken effect, which follows the opposite pattern. I gave little thought to it beyond this point, and just drank pale ale the rest of the trip, which is what I wanted to do anyway.

## The Coffee House

*Serves: 1 Specialty Cocktail, Breakfast, Lunch,
Specialty Coffees, Opens Early (6am)*

If your priorities and enthusiasms are anything like mine—rock-solid—it's always a delight when a new alcohol outlet pops up. The little Disneyland Hotel coffee shop is not new. It's been here for decades. What's new is how it now serves the coveted Dole Whip Rum Cocktail.

Used to be, this legendary tropical delicacy was available only at Walt Disney World. Even then, you had to either know about it and hunt for it. Then, to further the injustice, Disneyland finally got its own Trader Sam's, and we still couldn't get a Dole Cocktail.

Surely, the plan all along was to serve one of history's most sought-after sentimental beverages from a single, obscure coffee shop no one would know by name, or be able to find. No matter. If they served it in the parking garage, it would still be wonderful.

The Coffee House opens at 6am; even earlier on runDisney weekends. Anyone who gets themselves a Dole Whip Rum Cocktail at six in the morning, please send me a verifiable photo and a few words describing your motivation. I'll put you in the next book.

### What's to Drink

- Dole Whip with Rum

# Disney's Grand Californian Hotel & Spa

As an alternative or simply an addition to a day at the parks, the sprawling California-craftsman vacation paradise is your glorious, welcome retreat. The Grand Californian has been rendered only slightly less welcoming by the new security arrangement.

Guests staying on the west side of the resort, or who favor that end for parking could, historically, take advantage of the Grand Californian's convenient, picturesque access to Disneyland. From most points west, it meant quick access to the heart of Downtown Disney. From anywhere nearby, guests could enter Disney California Adventure skirting the worst of an often prolonged security bag check. Well, Disney caught on, and put a stop to that.

It's not that Disney wants to inconvenience anyone. Quite the contrary. The excess of well-informed outsiders have finally made matters more difficult for actual Grand Californian guests. As more of us filed into the hotel's semi-private access points, this supposed amenity for overnight guests degraded, and started to resemble the regular, more cumbersome entrances. Too bad, you say? Well, when you consider what it costs to stay at Disney's Grand Californian, those who foot the bill have good reason to expect a bit of special treatment.

Non-guests are no longer allowed onto the property through the front entrance on Disneyland Drive. It's going to take some getting used to. The access point was used by loads of visitors, and we all took pleasure in our widely shared little secret. You get your bags checked back by the ESPN Zone now. It frees up that terrible bottleneck at the west end of Disneyland's main entrance plaza, though does little to placate those of us who are shamefully turned back from the Grand Californian driveway.

If you find your way onto the property, either as a guest or through dogged persistence, spend some time here, even at the expense of some park exposure. I am slowly learning that time spent outside of Disneyland is not automatically, inherently wasted. I find it helps to remain on Disney property, engaged in Disney-related activities.

## *Hearthstone Lounge*

*Serves: Beer, Wine, Full Bar, Lunch, Dinner,*
*Specialty Drinks, Coffee, Opens Early*

Here we have a true gem, which becomes a less well-guarded secret with every passing day. Once was a time when you could slip into these charming cozy confines, have your pick of comfortable couches, and savor your coffee beverage of choice without waiting. Hearthstone is still charming, and comfortable, but now it's just a good deal more popular.

Table attrition is fairly consistent. You shouldn't have to wait long—that is, unless you want a coffee to go. The poor kids who work that end of the bar in the morning are a credit to Disney cast members everywhere.

I never like to step on toes, but when the servers are maxed out anyway, a delightful option is to get a drink from the bar and take it to the lobby. Disney's Grand Californian boasts "Craftsman-style elegance." Apparently, that means five-star woodland bungalow with a monorail going through it. The place is beautiful. I could amble the grounds, and, yes, simply sit in the lobby all day, if there weren't an equally enticing fun-park-resort also demanding my attention. As it is, once I sit down it would take a stampede of bison, or the Scottish Raspberry Lemon Drop to run out, to get me out of there.

### Featured Cocktails

#### Truffle Olive Martini

*Double Cross Vodka and Lillet Blanc Dry Vermouth, garnished with Truffle Olives*

#### Scottish Raspberry Lemon Drop

*Hendrick's Gin, Muddled Raspberries, fresh Lemon Juice, and Agave Nectar, topped with Wildberry Foam*

### Featured Brews (all 16oz draft)

- Karl Strauss Tower 10 IPA
- Anaheim Hefeweizen

## *Napa Rose Restaurant and Lounge*

*Serves: Beer, Wine, Full Bar, Lunch, Dinner, Specialty Drinks Menu*

One word: Joe. Without explanation, if you have even passed through the bar, you are aware of what a Disney-spirit-affirming cast member the Napa Rose has in Joe. For those who are unaware, visit the Napa Rose Lounge. Pray he is working.

Napa Rose boasts a world-renowned chef, perpetual five-diamond ratings, and a wine list that would impress Dionysius. Overarching, and ensuring, every memorable experience at this exquisite establishment is an unbelievable crew. Identifying one exemplary cast member is tantamount to choosing a favorite sunset. Within the pantheon of standouts, "the best" is a near meaningless designation. If I may play favorites, though, as that is what I have decided to do, Joe sits atop this truly select group.

Like Elizabeth at the Medocino Wine Terrace, you will find yourself looking for this cast member. When they're not there, your dinner, glass of wine, and evening will still be wonderful. But, it's a little like going to the park when the Matterhorn is closed. Space Mountain, the churros, fireworks, and your visit are all still amazing, but there's a little something missing. Also, just like with Elizabeth, I have to remind myself to be sensitive of their time. Joe, Elizabeth, and the splendid cast members like them are so generous with their attention, it's easy to lose yourself in their kindness. Delight in their expertise, soak up their spirit, and come back as often as you can. If you can remember to let them address and interact with other guests, you should probably do that as well.

### Featured Cocktails

#### Summer Kiss
*Hendrick's Gin, Combier, fresh Lemon Juice, St. Germain Elderflower Liqueur, and Absinthe Rinse*

#### The Happy Hungarian
*Zwack, Grand Marnier, Luxardo Gourmet Maraschino Cherries, Licor 43, fresh Lemon and Orange Juice, and Peychauds Bitters*

## Storytellers Café

*Serves: Beer, Wine, Full Bar, Breakfast, Lunch, Dinner, Opens Early*

We discussed proper character breakfast conduct above (see Goofy's Kitchen). All the same rules apply here, as you are likely to face all the same conditions. First, there will be children, everywhere. They will all be fired up to embark upon a brand-new Disney day, and the room full of their cartoon idols will surely exacerbate, well, everything.

If a banquet hall full of underage ruffians and giant mice, with bacon on the floor, would drive you to drink, then this is such a place. Please keep in mind the part about kids just trying to enjoy themselves at Disneyland. Some of those kids will be yours, or else what are you doing there, really?

If you weren't meant to drink at all, then you wouldn't be able to order from a full-service bar. Alcohol is not made available to test you. It is for you to enjoy. So, yeah, go right ahead. It is entirely possible to drink with full regard for your family. It's the completely sober guests who feel they can take all of the pineapple off the buffet with whom I have a problem.

Storytellers Café characters do not come out at lunchtime. Storytellers Café *does* serve alcohol at lunchtime. Knowing the preceding, know also it is a dirty rotten trick to bring your family here for lunch. Just because you want a cocktail, and some peace, does not justify luring your children into a character restaurant without any characters. There are other ways to trick your family, and get a drink, without breaking a child's heart. You can even do it entirely without their knowledge or scrutiny (see the "Disneyland Drinking Gymnastics" chapter).

## White Water Snacks

*Serves: Beer, Wine, Breakfast, Lunch, Dinner, Opens Early*

As exclusive service becomes more and more fleeting in the Hearthstone Lounge, the elusive and well-hidden White Water Snacks remains a much lesser-known treasure. You will not find glow cubes or IPA at this glorified snack bar, but there are always open tables, and almost never any line worth regretting.

When entering Disney California Adventure through the Grand Californian hotel gate, if you come to find a prohibitive line, White Water Snacks' welcoming arms are mere steps down the walkway. You can't take beer into the park, but you can certainly drink one while waiting for an inconvenient line to dwindle.

This particular park entrance is now a bit more difficult to access, given the new security arrangement. It's harder for most everyone to get here, so the line isn't as long. You can still grab a White Water snack and a drink, and contemplate how much simpler the world was when you could just pop over here from Katela Ave.

## What's to Drink
- Karl Strauss Amber Lager (not always available)
- Bud, Bud Light (16oz bottle)
- Coors Light (12oz bottle)
- Corona Extra (12oz bottle)

**Disney Drinking Tip.** If you want to get carded, ask for a Corona Extra. Adults drinking Corona do not order a Corona in this manner. It is an instant red flag for any server/bartender who is even mildly paying attention.

## Disney's Grand Californian Poolside
*Serves: Beer, Wine, Full Bar, Lunch, Dinner*

Disney's Grand Californian pool area is fairly standard for a Disneyland resort pool. That is to say, it is spectacular. Without resorting to criticism, the least inspiring Disney pool anywhere is a lap pool at the Walt Disney World Swan Hotel, and that, too, is delightful. People can, and do, spend entire days there, understandably.

For entertaining kids, gathering entire families, and appealing to grownups looking for a place to hang out, Disney's Grand Californian swim complex offers something for everyone. There's beverage service at the pool itself, so it at least has something for adults looking to get catered to.

You need to be staying at the Californian to get through the pool gate. We all know there are ways around that, though I implore you never to break even unwritten Disney rules. As the guy who thought putting wine into a Dasani bottle would be enough to fool Disney security, I haven't the strongest foundation upon which to dispense such an admonition. So, if you are staying here, or manage to get in and promise to behave yourself, dip your feet in any of the pools without the slide—they're more relaxing—and let a charming Disney cast member deliver an IPA directly into your eager grasp.

Presently (mid 2017), the entire place is undergoing a major remodel. How do you improve upon something that's already exemplary? Well, you leave it in Disney's creative and capable hands. Excited to see what results. As I suspect the patio furniture to be as comfortable, and plentiful, as it was before the remodel, I expect to be pleased, if I can get in.

### Acorns Gifts and Goods
*Sells: Beer, Wine*

If you are among the truly blessed who can actually stay at a Disneyland hotel, but aren't industrious enough to travel with your own wine or beer, you're in luck. Lobby gift shops, including at Disney's Grand Californian, sell both.

You will get much better beer in Hearthstone Lounge, and far finer wine from Napa Rose. If you try to take six beverages from those places to your room, people are going to look at you funny. Acorn Gifts is a convenient way to top off your shopping, and cap off your night, with far less scrutiny.

The next step is to make sure you don't ever forget to get booze for your hotel room again. With a little planning you could be sitting on the deck of your glorious California Craftsman-style palatial suite, with your favorite drink in hand. Instead, you have Bud Light. Better than nothing, but I hope you've learned your lesson.

### What's to Drink
- Red, White, Blush Wines by the bottle
- Blue Moon (12oz bottle)
- Corona (12oz bottle)
- Heineken (12oz bottle)
- Bud Light (12oz bottle)
- Coors Light (12oz bottle)

# Disney's Paradise Pier Hotel

Paradise Pier is an under-appreciated resort, though only among people who have never stayed here. Not an original Disney property, this glorious hotel does not get the respect it warrants. Enjoy a dance party with Stitch, an IPA in a life-saving lounge chair, or catch the World of Color from the right room, and you'll quickly come around. Stop in for a meal, or simply because you were turned away from using Disney's Grand Californian's former secret entrance.

## Disney's PCH Grill

*Serves: Beer, Wine, Full Bar, Breakfast, Dinner,*
*Specialty Drinks, Open Early*

A third character-themed restaurant in as many hotels. See Goofy's Kitchen, and perhaps a rehabilitation specialist.

All of the character restaurants have their particular charm and personality. Goofy's has the chef motif, and Goofy, of course. Ariel's has the parade of princesses. The PCH Grill sets itself apart with a wholly spectacular California dance party. It's loud, it's frequent, and it is positively a participation endeavor. Children are drawn to it like little frolicking moths. When Stitch comes out and starts jammin' to "Surfin' Safari," I swear kids come in from off the street to join in.

If you have been placed at any of the tables lining the dance area, which is essentially half the restaurant, I caution you to be prepared. By this, I mean order a Bloody Mary as you sit down. If Stitch doesn't get you on the dance floor, be ready for him to join you at your table. It's a buffet so at some point there will be an open seat, and he's going to take it, and probably your bacon.

It's delightful. All of the character meals are. Mickey Mouse makes regular, lengthy appearances, as do many of his popular buddies. If these things weren't over the top and distracting, they wouldn't be serving their purpose. Try to endure it with patience, and not more than three mimosas—though I defy you to try it with zero.

## Surfside Lounge

*Serves: Beer, Wine, Full Bar, Breakfast, Lunch,*
*Dinner, Specialty Drinks, Opens Early*

It is always wise to make a reservation for a character meal. You don't always get right in, even when you have one. Turning up without a reservation is an exercise in frustration, and you can see groups of such people, contemplating this very fact, standing outside of every character restaurant.

It's no coincidence, then, that every character restaurant has a lounge nearby. So, you can post up at the door, frowning at the hosts, watching as no progress is made on the wait list, or you can retreat to the bar and commit to making reservations in the future. Consider yourself fortunate if you have made this blunder at PCH Grill or Goofy's Kitchen. Those bar lounges are right there. At Storytellers, it's not far off, but it's doubtful you will hear them call your name. At Ariel's, it's not that the Cove Bar is so far away, but during breakfast it's not open, and the rest of the day you'll have trouble getting in. Picture that joyous prospect: faced with an hour wait for your character meal, you get to weather the slings and arrows of your outraged children, and the nearest bar has its own insufferable wait.

If you aren't keen enough to plan ahead, hopefully you're lucky enough to be over at Disney's Paradise Pier Hotel. In the padded seating in the lounge, your children can watch cartoons, you can hear when your name is called, and in the intervening hour or so, an accommodating Surfside Lounge cast member will construct and hand you drinks.

## Mickey in Paradise Gifts

*Sells: Beer, Wine*

Few pleasures delight a traveling adult quite like checking into a hotel that has a lounge with a bar in it. Okay, checking into any Disneyland resort carries with it several layers of amazing that have more to do with Mickey Mouse, fireworks, magic, and two parks full of roller coasters than any bar, but the traveling adults know what I mean.

Another blessing is a gift shop—especially a gift shop that sells beer and wine, and which keeps longer hours than the bar.

It's no Costco. That is to say, the selection is not mind blowing, though the prices may be. You are paying for convenience here. And considering you would be paying a dollar more for a Coors Light right across the hallway, were the lounge open, there's very little to complain about—unless it's that you shouldn't be drinking Coors Light.

**Disney Drinking Tip.** Despite what I just said, if you are drinking in Surfside Lounge, Hearthstone, or Steakhouse 55, do not make beer runs to the gift shop. Yes, it makes financial sense, especially if you are content with the shop's beer selection. Nothing delights a server or bartender more than a guest taking up one of their precious seats, but not buying anything. Even Disney cast members, the world's leading customer-service providers, would take a dim view of this.

### What's to Drink
- Red, White, Sparkling White, Blush Wines by the bottle
- Blue Moon (12oz bottle)
- Corona (12oz bottle)
- Heineken (12oz bottle)
- Bud Light (16oz bottle)
- Coors Light (16oz bottle)

## *Paradise Pier Poolside*

Paradise Pier has a delightful pool complex. It is on top of the fifth-floor roof of the hotel's west wing. There is an impressive water slide, and some of the time there is a full-service grill with adult beverages. It is really difficult to predict the pool bar's hours of operation. When the wind blows from the wrong direction, or with a few too many clouds in the sky, everyone but the lifeguard disappears.

You are allowed to bring drinks to the pool, in the proper plasticware, if you can convince the kid with the whistle you purchased them at the lounge or gift shop. You are absolutely not allowed to use the waterslide when the attendant is not there. Do not ask me how I know this. It has a little to do with beverages from the lounge, and was not my proudest moment.

CHAPTER FOUR

# Drinking at Downtown Disney

There will be times when you find yourself at the Disneyland Resort, though will not have cause, time, or passes to be inside the parks. Try to limit those instances. Go in, ride some rides. Downtown Disney is a delightful refuge for those on the fringe, who still want to experience the magic, but are too cheap to buy tickets.

Downtown Disney is a convenient, attractive alternative to occasionally interminable wait times for food at Disneyland. There is a blessed wealth of places to eat and to get a drink. In deference to Epcot's Drinking Around the World participants, do not try to hit all the bars in one visit.

Most Downtown restaurants also feature a full bar. My editor, an understanding and generous individual, would not be impressed with my rehashing every available beer, wine, and booze bottle, so several favorites, staples, and interesting highlights are listed for each location. Though I don't mention them all specifically, you are quite safe assuming every bar has Smirnoff and Coors Light. Don't order either, but, sure, expect them to be there.

## Catal Restaurant
*Serves: Beer, Wine, Full Bar, Breakfast, Lunch, Dinner,*
*Opens Early (public bar opens at noon), Happy Hour*

If you are celebrating something, didn't make Napa Rose reservations, and choose not to walk all the way to Steakhouse 55, Catal Restaurant is an exquisite intermediary. This is not the type of place you are going to stumble up to and have a drink, however. It's so nice as to be a little bit intimidating. Luckily, there's a lounge upstairs with a bar in it. Whether you're waiting on a table, your reservation, or just realize you're a little under-dressed for the dining room, Catal still caters to us. Just try to behave yourself.

As if you weren't already intimidated, the lounge isn't even mentioned on the Disneyland website. It's as luxurious as the rest of the impeccable restaurant. When I found out they have Karl Strauss Mosaic Session IPA on tap, I was able to relax completely.

For all the times you've walked through Downtown Disney and wondered what it takes to get one of those obviously privileged tables on the second story of several of the establishments, the Catal lounge can be your ticket—unless, of course, they aren't seating outside for the lounge, which does happen. No one will disclose the official policy.

The restaurant itself offers a full-service bar, beginning at breakfast, although the bar itself won't yet be open. If you can wait until noon, and just want a drink, while lounging in luxury, the bar is noteworthy. I imagine you will still receive courteous service if you show up in shorts and funny hats, with a bunch of kids and packages. I haven't tried it, didn't see anyone else doing it, and can't recommend it.

Draft beer, several wine varieties, and some signature cocktails are $7 (at press time) on happy hour, 3–5pm, everyday. It's quite exceptional to even offer a discount at a place like this. What makes it an even better deal, I first stumbled into Catal's happy hour on the heels of learning Naples Ristorante, nearby, charges $40 for a pitcher of beer. My math is spotty, but it seemed I could get six of Catal's massive, wonderful beers for the same price. After my third beer, my math became even less reliable than my attention span, and I forgot entirely what had gotten me so worked up.

## *Featured Cocktails*

### Vojito
*Absolut Vodka, Berries, Lime Juice, Mint, Agave Nectar, Soda Water*

### Cucumber Martini
*Effen Cucumber Vodka, Lime Juice, Agave Nectar, fresh Mint, Cucumber*

"The Duke" Old Fashioned
*Russel's Reserve Rye 6yr Whiskey, Bitters, Orange, Cherry*

### *Featured Brews*

- Karl Strauss Mosaic Session IPA (16oz draft)
- Left Coast Catal Blonde Draft (16oz draft)
- Modern Times Black House (16oz draft)
- Ballast Point Grapefruit Sculpin (12oz bottle)

# Earl of Sandwich

*Serves: Beer, Wine, Breakfast, Lunch, Dinner, Opens Early*

I am loathe to recommend leaving the parks for any reason other than their closing. Incredible food options are an exception. Earl of Sandwich has become an oasis in times of need, hunger, and crowd relief. No offense to anything else purely Disney, but this is the most affordable spot in the whole resort to get a substantial, healthy, enviable meal without a ridiculous wait. And they sell beer.

Aside from grabbing a roadie at one of the hotel gift shops, this might well be your best option for getting in that early morning beverage. Anywhere you get a breakfast beer, you are going to invite scrutiny. People have a blind spot for the glorious tradition, and I feel for them. At a theme park, which caters to children, some pushback is probably appropriate and healthy.

Day drinking at Disneyland should come at an emotional as well as a financial price, or people will be more apt to abuse it. I prefer to face the judgment of the fine people at Earl of Sandwich, rather than the cast at a character breakfast. Neither is going to overtly ruin your day. A knowing glance at Earl of Sandwich just seems preferable to a piteous look from Chip, Dale, or Princess Tiana. When a fully festooned costume character is so disappointed in you that you can feel it through their mask, fur, and floppy ears, it's not something you get over quickly.

Earl of Sandwich will, at times, have a line, but it moves well. The sandwich artisans are courteous and efficient. Seating is ample, if you don't mind occasionally sharing part of a table beirgarten-style. It's a nice way to meet people, and is how I discovered they serve Pacifico. Yes, to my shame, the first couple times I went to Earl of Sandwich, it was exclusively to eat. When the kindly couple sitting across the table, who I tried to covertly acknowledge for successfully sneaking beer into the dining area, informed me they bought beer at the cash register, out in the open and everything, my world changed.

Be aware that you get to buy a bottle, but you don't get to keep it. Downtown Disney does not permit guests to walk around with alcohol, so the plastic cup is not an invitation to wander. By invitation or otherwise, Security knows there are those who are going to do it anyway. Earl of Sandwich wants to make sure you don't stray with a glass bottle in your hand.

### What's to Drink

- Bud, Bud Light (12oz bottle)
- Pacifico Cervesa (12oz bottle)
- Corona (12oz bottle)
- Stella Artois (12oz bottle)
- Barefoot Sauvignon Blanc, Cabernet, Merlot

# ESPN Zone

*Serves: Beer, Wine, Full Bar, Lunch Dinner,*
*Open Late (11:00am– 11:00pm)*

Certain Downtown Disney restaurants can be overwhelming. ESPN Zone, now towering over the newly relocated western-entrance security bag check, is the district's hyperactive little brother. It is like an elementary school at lunchtime, but with more televisions. It's a blast, if you're looking for a raucous following for a favored sports team. If you'd rather have a spot to relax after a long day's park hopping, this ain't it.

Sports fans are well aware of ESPN Zone, and also know what to expect. They are incredible venues to catch a game. Regardless of the time of year, or your sport of choice, you will always find an enthusiastic fan base, willing to back both sides of any contest. As with most worthwhile sports bars, this can be a rough spot to be if your team is a perennial winner, but isn't winning that particular night. Luke-warm spectators tend to gravitate toward the hardcore fans who will enthusiastically root against a front-runner. I have no empathy for Patriot, Yankee, Cavalier, and Manchester fans, though offer these words of caution about looking for outside support at an ESPN Zone: you won't find any.

You will find three full, high-energy bars, a massive dining room, and an arcade wonderland. From any seat or air hockey table in the house, you can see a huge handful of TVs. So, if you've come to watch a game, your options are numerous. If you have come as part of a family, can I implore you to choose the restaurant or arcade?

Bar service is historically efficient, and rare is the need to put your name in to secure bar seating. When all you want to do is drink, perhaps have nachos, and catch a game that they won't be airing on the one TV in the Catal lounge, and you walk in to face a bar full of children, and no open seating, even the most understanding sports fan can become dispirited.

Disney is all about family. This cannot be overstated. Just know that not a single server in the dining room wouldn't rather have families churning through their section versus tables full of sedentary single guys who aren't eating. I am a fair tipper, but you aren't going to make rent with people like me occupying all your four-tops for the duration of an entire football game.

Disney guests don't like to fritter away valuable park time. When your family walks into the ESPN foyer to see a line snaking toward the restaurant, then that open and inviting tunnel to the right leading to the bar, the choice is obvious. I understand the motivation, but if you have an open seat at your bar table when I walk in during the playoffs, don't be surprised if I join you.

**Disney Drinking Tip.** The televisions in the ESPN bathrooms are a courtesy to guests who are using the restroom, while using the restroom. You are not meant to hang out there and watch games—especially not, and yes, this needs to be said, not over anyone's shoulder. To the person who did that the other night, you creeped me out. When you tried to engage me in conversation, you just made it worse.

## Featured Cocktails

### The Espy
*Myers's Platinum Rum, Cruzan Black Cherry Rum, Captain Morgan Original Spiced Rum, Wildberry, and Sprite*

### MVP Margarita
*Don Julio Silver Tequila, Grand Marnier, fresh Lime Juice, and Agave Nectar*

### Ultimate Bloody Mary
*Ketel One Vodka featuring Demetri's All Natural Classic Recipe Bloody Mary Seasoning*

### Vanilla Russian
*Smirnoff Vanilla Twist Vodka, Godiva Chocolate Liqueur, and Baileys Original Irish Cream*

## *Featured Brews*

- Stone IPA (16oz draft)
- Karl Strauss Pintail Pale Ale (16oz draft)
- Ballast Point Sculpin IPA (12oz bottle)
- Bud Light (16oz draft or 12oz bottle)
- Coors Light (16oz draft or 12oz bottle)

# House of Blues, Anaheim

At press time, the Downtown Disney House of Blues is a literal smoking hole in the ground. The charming concert venue has moved down the block a bit, to clear a path for a West Coast Splitsville Bowling Alley. If it is anything like the Disney Springs Splitsville at Walt Disney World (it will be), we are blessed. I enjoyed House of Blues immensely. The bar, food, and service were terrific. An Anaheim Splitsville will make it hard to miss.

# La Brea Bakery Cafe and Express

*Serves: Beer, Wine, Full Bar, Breakfast, Lunch, Dinner, Opens Early*

This is the closest place to the Disneyland entrance plaza to get an adult beverage. If you are of a mind to take advantage of it, know it requires putting your name in for table service. If you ran out of the park, in a mad panic, in hopes of a quick drink from the express line, I've got bad news. Perhaps it is because of the convenient proximity, and they don't want panicked guests popping in and out of Disneyland for drinks, but La Brea Express does not sell alcohol.

The restaurant *does* serve alcohol. Indeed, they serve rather delicious Bloody Marys. There is an actual bar. It appears guests are expected to wait their turn, then sit there and eat, if they so desire. You are not, I learned to my shame, meant to walk up and order a beverage to go. Again, it likely has a lot to do with being so close to the historically family-friendly theme park.

One can argue that La Brea is no closer to the esplanade than Carthay Circle. They might be right, if disagreeable. You do have the extra Disney California Adventure gate with which to contend. Carthay doesn't open as early, and does tend to develop a line, which will limit ambitious park hoppers on a beer run.

La Brea would be the perfect fallback, then. Disney surely anticipated this, and squashed it. Can't fault or blame them. Family first, right? There was a time when I would never recommend waiting for a table, just to get a drink, especially at Disneyland. Between La Brea's Bloody Mary with Tajin in it, the Grand Marnier Margarita, and Stone Delicious IPA, I won't fault anyone who chooses to hang out awhile.

## Featured Cocktails

### La Brea Bakery Bloody Mary
*Skyy Vodka, all-natural Bloody Mary mix, Tajin rim*

### Classic Caddy Margarita
*Sauza 100% Blue Agave Tequila, fresh Juices, Grand Marnier Float, salted rim*

### Moscow Mule
*Skyy Vodka, Lime Juice, Ginger Beer, Bitters*

### Bellini
*Sparkling Wine, Peach Puree*

## Featured Brews (all 16oz draft)

- Racer 5 IPA
- Blood Orange Wit
- Stella, Bud Light

- Stone Delicious IPA
- Yeti Imperial Stout
- White Rascal Belgium Ale

# Naples Ristorante e Pizzeria
*Serves: Beer, Wine, Full Bar, Lunch, Dinner, Happy Hour*

Downtown Disney's popularity is undeniable. On any given day, every restaurant may have a wait for a table. Disney is not in the business of frustrating its guests, and they positively encourage the mostly independent businesses of the Downtown Disney District to follow their lead. In this vein, every Downtown Disney table-service restaurant also features a bar, lounge, or alternative quick-service option. Given its wonderful food and proximity to Disneyland's main gate, Naples opted for both a bar and a quick-service annex.

Naples also offers an unexpected Happy Hour. Monday through Friday, 3–5pm, beer, wine, and a couple delicious appetizers are available at an attractive discount. House wine and 16oz draft beer are each $7 (at press time) during happy hour. A $7 beer may not cause you to stampede over here every day of your visit, nor should it. I'm always going to recommend heading into Disney California Adventure, over diverting Downtown, for drinks or otherwise. But, if you aren't park hopping, considering how close Naples is to Disneyland's main gate, you could well salvage your vacation if you are in the right place as 3 o'clock approaches.

***Disney Drinking Tip.*** Within Disneyland, if you are not park hopping, and if you want to be covertly within striking distance of a certain Downtown Disney destination when happy hour rolls around, take full advantage of the mtonorail and the Disneyland Railroad. The railroad is closed until Star Wars Land opens at a future date, a long, long time from now. This advice will be good again when it returns, and these monorail tips are evergreen. From pretty much anywhere in the park, if you trek deliberately toward the front gate, anyone in your party who has even been there twice is going to catch on. As soon as you turn down Main Street, unless you have lunch reservations at Carnation Café, your party will be brimming with suspicion. At that point you are either headed shopping, to Great Moments with Mr. Lincoln, or you're leaving. If you hop on the monorail, you can conceivably be finishing a Rainforest Piña Colada before your family knows what you're up to.

## What's to Drink (all 16oz draft)

- Moretti
- Angel City IPA
- Samuel Adams Seasonal
- Stella Artois
- Negra Modelo
- Fat Tire
- Shock Top
- Bud, Bud Light

# Napolini

*Serves: Beer, Wine, Lunch, Dinner*

Similar to La Brea Bakery Express, across the way, Napolini is a convenient spot to grab a quick bite and a sanity-salvaging beverage. You can't walk through Downtown Disney with alcohol, so don't expect to take a Shock Top to go. There aren't a ton of tables. Who can blame you, then, for crouching behind the soda dispenser to drink a beer in relative peace?

Napolini has the most diverse beverage selection of any Downtown Disney quick-service option. Even if they don't have exactly what you're looking for, they will have something close. They also sell full bottles of wine. I have to assume that is for people ordering full meals and who plan to stay awhile. I have, as yet, not attempted to buy one on my own and drink it, furtively, behind the soda machine. That's a stretch, even for me.

***Disney Drinking Tip.*** The family members you left outside, with the assumption you have gone into Napolini to use the restroom and steal parmesan packets, will be able to see you, if you aren't thinking strategically. More to the point, if you don't want your people to know you've slipped in for a beer, the soda machine provides excellent cover. You will want to be courteous to anyone around you who is simply just trying to get a soda. Also, have a backup excuse ready for when your annoyingly attentive child points out the Starbucks across the walkway has restrooms, too.

### What's to Drink

- Marlborough, Savignon Blanc, 750ml
- Bellini
- Stella Artois (12oz bottle)
- Fat Tire (12oz bottle)
- Guinness (12oz bottle)
- Negra Modelo (12oz bottle)
- Angry Orchard (12oz bottle)

# Rainforest Café

*Serves: Beer, Wine, Full Bar, Breakfast, Lunch, Dinner, Opens Early*

If your plan is to retreat for a Downtown Disney District dinner, to escape the bustle and high pulse of the parks, we can't think of a worse place to do it. Rainforest Café is thrilling. The service is over-the-top wonderful. It will provide no relief at all. You'd be better off eating in Toontown, or while riding Splash Mountain (do not attempt).

Just to get near Rainforest you have to negotiate squawking birds, a live band, fountains, and pyrotechnics. And that's all before you wrestle your way through the crowd to be told by the kids in the giant elephant head that there's an eighty-minute wait for a table. By the time you do get a table, you ought to be so sufficiently frazzled, you will likely start drinking, even if you hadn't previously intended to. I had a bucket of Sierra Nevada here one night. If it didn't take forty minutes to get it, I think it would have gone a long way toward mollifying my shattered nerves and mood. I do not blame our server for the delay. I think our table was on the third-floor roof. The only animals that were visible to us were mountain goats. I think they were real, and native to that remote section of the restaurant.

Readers of this book ought to be more apt to seek out a table in the bar. Those, too, are difficult to come by, and are similarly surrounded by the mayhem. For an establishment the size of this particular Rainforest Café, the bar is tiny. After shoehorning in the animatronic animals, aquarium, arboretum, elevator, and gift shop, apparently there wasn't room for much else.

The best way to enjoy a drink at Rainforest is at breakfast. (I know, early drinking at Disneyland is a recipe for ruining a day at Disneyland.) The Rainforest Bloody Mary is called Jungle Fever. It's deliciously spicy and comes with kettle chips.

Want to get your Disney day off to a bewildering start? Get a massive, exotic coffee at Starbucks, then go to Rainforest for breakfast. The crowds are much more manageable, but all the fun and frivolity is still going on in the restaurant. It rains. Wild animals jump out of the walls and ceiling. A Jungle Fever or two, to cap off breakfast, and you're ready to face the Disneyland Resort like a first-time visitor. Enjoy the parks like the amateurs do: distracted, directionless, and with little intentional influence on what you are going to accomplish that day.

### *Featured Cocktails*

#### Green Python
*SKYY Infused Citrus Vodka, Midori Melon Liqueur, Don Q Coconut Rum, 99 Bananas Liqueur, Sweet & Sour, Pineapple Juice*

#### Dragonberry Mule
*Bacardi Dragon Berry Rum, St-Germain Elderflower Liqueur, Strawberry Purée, Ginger Beer, fresh Lime Juice*

# Ralph Brennan's Jazz Kitchen & Express

*Serves: Beer, Wine, Full Bar, Lunch, Dinner*

I love the theme, food, staff, and atmosphere of this restaurant. Every time I have been in the bar, I get claustrophobic. This is probably no one's fault. But, the bar is either too crowded when I am there, or it's cramped to the point of a design flaw. It's the kind of place I should love. The live entertainment is absolutely my bag. They serve draft beer by the litre, and offer Arbita Wrought Iron IPA.

A note on drinking beer by the litre at a jazz bar, or anywhere, really. For an American, a litre is rather a deceptive means of measuring beer. We are conditioned to monitor our own consumption in very specific 12-ounce beer units. At any point during a night out, tedious lecture, or tailgate party, when you ask your friend how many beers they've had, they can reply with complete confidence, if not total accuracy. But, they will know, and you will know, and everything makes sense. Most important, everyone may carry on drinking with at least moderate certainty that no one is in eminent, terminal danger.

Ralph Brennan's serves several delicious draft brews by the glass, or litre. Even if you are some kind of freak, and can convert litres to beers in your head, how long into a litre-swilling evening are you going to be able to continue such sorcery? Besides which, Brennan litre beers come in a carafe. Anyone can count bottles, but carafes? You'll lose focus just trying to pour the thing without spilling on the people at the next table.

Further confusing matters, and your group of friends, the prices are inconsistent. Rather, they follow a well-ordered pattern, just in a manner that compels you to drink more. Your first carafe, whatever that is, is $16. Each following litre is $12. No matter how many beers are in a litre, everyone knows you have to get that second one to bring the costs down. The truly fiscally minded understand that with each successive carafe, the first one becomes progressively more reasonable. You may have no idea how much you've had, or even where you are anymore, but you'll be darned if you are going to let a little thing like the metric system, or alcohol poisoning, keep you from a good deal.

Still, I always feel more comfortable at a table here. This often requires quite a wait, and means you'd better be ordering food. The menu is so full of authentic delicacies, I don't mind. The other good news: you can get litre beers at the table.

## *What's to Drink*

- Arbita Wrought Iron IPA (16oz draft)
- Karl Strauss Tower 10 IPA (12oz bottle)
- Stone Ruination IPA (12oz bottle)
- Cabotella (12oz bottle)

# Tortilla Jo's Resturante

*Serves: Beer, Wine, Full Bar, Breakfast, Lunch, Dinner (11am–10pm)*

Between the restaurant, cantina, and quick-service taqueria, if Tortilla Jo's was the only Downtown Disney District establishment, I'd be perfectly happy. Of course, that's ridiculous, as it would mean no Earl of Sandwich, and Jo's would be crowded beyond all practical patronage, but those who have been here know what I mean.

A Mexican restaurant in the middle of Downtown Disney, asked to cater to American tastes, cannot compare to your neighborhood favorite. They have free chips and salsa and an excellent cerveza selection, so focus on that and enjoy yourself.

# Tortilla Jo's Taqueria

*Serves: Beer (12oz), Margaritas, Breakfast, Lunch, Dinner, Opens Early (8am–11pm)*

If you are used to quality quick-service Mexican food, you are going to want to adjust your expectations. Tortilla Jo's has good food, it's just not fair to compare it to the family-owned cocina from your old neighborhood.

What Tortilla Joe's Taqueria does have is a hearty menu of reasonably priced food, considering it's in the middle of a relatively high-end shopping mall. It also has the quickest moving line this side of Pirates of the Caribbean. When you're hungry during the peak season, relax your standards somewhat, painlessly get something to eat, and enjoy an excellent Mexican beer (Negra Modelo).

### What's to Drink

- Negra Modelo (12oz bottle)
- Pacifico (12oz bottle)
- Corona, Corona Light (12oz bottle)
- Budweiser (12oz bottle)
- Coors Light (12oz bottle)
- Lime, Strawberry Frozen Margaritas

# Uva Bar

*Serves: Beer, Wine, Full Bar, Lunch, Dinner, Open Late*

Literally, figuratively, and geographically, Uva Bar is an island of refreshment in the sea of magic and fluid humanity.

There aren't but three days a year in Anaheim that aren't suitable for outside patio bar enjoyment. If you happen to be at the Disneyland Resort on an off day, then come back tomorrow, and go to the Uva Bar. It's exactly the type of patio most suited for all your leisurely needs. Acres of bar space, loads of tables, umbrellas, heaters, and plenty of space in between to let the sun shine in.

Downtown Disney pulses around the bar like an artery, including the highly trafficked pedestrian thoroughfare. Disneyland features legendary people watching. For this, particularly, Uva ranks up there with the green benches at the Hub-end of Main Street. And until they start serving Bloody Marys in Disneyland, Uva is a comparable place to hang out.

The draft beer selection rivals Disney California Adventure's distribution truck. Currently, they are pouring Karl Strauss Aurora Hoppyalis and Ballast Point Sculpin; two of our local favorites. The bar staff is attentive and amicable. If Uva wasn't so shamefully close to Disneyland, I would spend a lot more time here, with far less guilt.

## *Featured Cocktails*

**Breakfast Bloody Mary**
*Housemade Bloody Mary mix, Vodka, Celery, Bacon*

**Strawberry Fizz**
*Gin, Lime Juice, Agave Nectar, Strawberry, Mint*

# CHAPTER FIVE

# Disneyland Drinking Gymnastics

Disney does not have to serve alcohol. Not anywhere. Not on any of its properties. If it weren't such a massive money-maker, they probably wouldn't. Disney is hardly at a loss for other ways to drive revenue. Movie theaters have thrived for generations without alcohol. True, the neighborhood theater is now giving way to the full-service megaplex, but I suspect we are reaching the upper limit for how much American audiences are willing to pay for a night at the cinema.

I also suspect, at their quarterly meetings, Disney execs regularly weigh the wisdom of continuing to mix alcohol into their family-oriented enterprise. I don't believe we will see dry Disney campuses in our lifetimes. But, if the example I'm about to relate, involving the band Off Kilter, is any indication, when drinking-related pursuits threaten to taint the historically wholesome brand, Disney will favor the latter, regardless of the popularity of the former.

Off Kilter is an astoundingly entertaining Celtic rock band. For years, Off Kilter thrilled Walt Disney World audiences with multiple daily stage shows at Epcot's World Showcase Events Pavilion. Guests would sing, dance, and delight to traditional tunes, energetic musical performances, and crowd-contributed whimsy. Then, on the heels of an 18-year run, Disney pulled the plug.

Disney's official position was a need to revamp their live entertainment. Off Kilter's enormous, consistent following belies such dubious reasoning. When the lumberjack show that replaced them proved untenable, and they didn't bring Off Kilter back, Disney's true motivation proved difficult to dispute.

Droves of locals would visit Walt Disney World Resort exclusively to see Off Kilter. They are that type of group. They also put on the kind of show you can enjoy on a much more enthusiastic level with a couple pints in you. What you regularly had, then, was this massive, fervent gathering in the middle of the World Showcase, too often, mostly blocking a vital Epcot pedestrian artery.

It wasn't difficult for Disney to determine Off Kilter's groupies were mostly outside of their key marketing demographic. Epcot could count on fairly consistent beer sales surrounding Off Kilter performances. But, if you aren't visiting as a member of a true money-spending family, and you are creating a hindrance for those who are, change is going to come.

Many are astounded Disney would walk away from something so vastly popular. It's only really shocking if you think Disney is not aware how popularity doesn't always fill cash registers. The joyous, respectfully raucous shows are a tragic loss, but it's not difficult to appreciate Disney's position.

Much of the Off Kilter audience consisted of local annual passholders and off-duty cast members, the people least likely to spend gobs of extra money. This is not a criticism. Local, regular visitors, and especially cast members, are most keen on ways to do Walt Disney World for the least amount of money. If this contingent happens to be in the way of others, reducing others' willingness to hang around and spend money, Disney's choice becomes simple, even if unpopular.

We can also assume the Epcot executives and security personnel are aware of those who drink before they arrive, and those who make personal beer runs to the parking lot (you know who you are). These people are even less likely to spend money in the park. Even if it isn't blocking an important walkway, and complicating family patronage, Disney cannot forever cater to a drunken mass with essentially free entertainment. I miss Off Kilter, too. But, unless there were some politics or semantics I am unaware of—entirely possible—the fault for their removal lies more with us, the tight-fisted groupies, than with Disney.

This may seem like sacrilege, but alcohol is the least important aspect of your Disney vacation or visit. Time at Disneyland is rare, even for those who go often. You can get a drink pretty much anywhere else you go, every single other day of your life. How many of those other places have a Space Mountain?

Take full advantage of your time. And by that, I'm saying do not sacrifice any element of your Disneyland Resort visit for alcohol. Don't pass on an attraction. Don't skip dinner. Don't forgo Disneyland itself just because there's no beer. All that said, there is no reason you can't wisely incorporate an adult beverage, or two, or as many as you can handle, while remaining a rational, unobtrusive adult, into your delightful Disney day.

If you are not visiting Disneyland with family, you can still benefit from the attached advice. Everywhere I refer to family, insert "that friend who doesn't drink as much as you." Perhaps you have even learned what a pleasure it can be to spend a day at Disneyland on your own. Truly, it is. Those who are unaware of this likely have never tried it. When visiting alone, then, consider the friendly security agents in the white hats part of your extended, extremely attentive family.

FASTPASSes and the Disney California Adventure guide map are crucial for maximum enjoyment for you and your family. They're free. Maps are available at every park gate, while FASTPASS now accompanies every attraction you would ever want to ride, except Alice and Peter Pan. With these tools you may strike the perfect balance between wholesome family fun and appropriate adult fulfillment. I'm here to teach you how.

Consider, you have been at the park for six hours. You are standing in front of Heimlich's Chew Chew Train. It currently has a fifteen-minute wait. Disney veterans will instantly observe how crowded the park must be on this day. "a bug's land," generally, and Heimlich in particular, get crowded last. If "a bug's land" is that busy, you've probably had a rough six hours. You could probably use a drink.

When your party suggests getting into the fifteen-minute line, it's time to draw upon your fortuitous map and park savvy. With enthusiasm, suggest that while they ride Heimlich, you will go get FASTPASSES for Soarin'. It is vital you sell this with the proper conviction. Make them feel you are genuinely sorry to miss the hopelessly charming burping-caterpillar ride, yet are wholly committed to securing a shorter wait for a more highly valued family attraction. Imply that you are going to miss them, for good measure. Don't be overly dramatic about this. Overdo it and everyone is going to know you're just bugging out for a beer.

If you pull it off, you have bought yourself roughly 25 minutes of freedom. Rejoice, but do not go completely off the rails. If you come back without FASTPASSES, or at least some convincing excuse, you are going to blow the entire operation. It'll be sobriety and excessive standby lines for you the rest of the way.

Continuing with this specific example, the walk to Soarin' from "a bug's land" and back can be accomplished in less than ten minutes. With your map, identify locations on the route that serve the kind of beer you like. Picking the closest will afford you the luxury of having a beer as you make your way over to Grizzly Peak. Waiting until later in your journey will help you not get spotted by your family. It will, however, make it more difficult to take advantage of Soarin's proximity to Smokejumpers Grill, where you will want to grab another beverage on your way back.

I am not suggesting anyone attempt to drink two beers in the brief trip between "a bug's land" and Grizzly Peak. (Never mind that is exactly what I have instructed you to do.) I am just describing how it is possible, if you plan properly. But, no, of course don't do that, especially if your family is waiting to enjoy your presence and participation once you return.

With these shenanigans now implanted in your brain, you will begin to plot your own side adventures. Just don't go getting overly ambitious. "Hey," you're now thinking, "I bet I can get from Monsters, Inc. to Radiator Springs and back by the time my unsuspecting family gets off that ride."

This does illustrate rare brilliance. Racer 5, Tower 10, Schweiger Cabernet, and Fillmore's Pomegranate Limeade are all sold on that route. But this strategy has several problems.

First, it's farther than it looks on the map. You may well get there and back, but you won't have time to enjoy even a single drink. Okay, if you're hustling, you can pop into Flo's and buy one. Good luck drinking it at a jog, while weaving through Disney guests unsympathetic to your plight.

Next, if your plan involves stopping at Carthay Circle, there could well be a line. Even when there isn't, it can take longer than you expect to get served. The service is wonderful, but expect that a fair amount of people got there before you. Expect them also to be hung up on the menu, and more interested in taking in the charming decor than placing a quick order to help you scam your family.

Your children are also likely aware exactly when Radiator Springs Racers FASTPASS distribution closes. Forgetting this bit of information, yourself, will win you a sober sojourn on Monsters, Inc., with your now rightly suspicious family.

Many ambitious Disney drinkers wander unwittingly into another pitfall: the inter-park FASTPASS -retrieval blunder. The huge window you might be afforded by convincing your party to let you secure FASTPASSes in the alternate park is rarely as wide open, or smoothly transitioned, as it appears on paper.

Yes, if you're kids are queued up to see Minnie Mouse in Toontown, and you offer to get California Screamin' passes, you can theoretically be gone for up to an hour before anyone starts missing or texting you in earnest. The sheer quantity of adult refreshment lining that route presents a nigh irresistible temptation. Successfully being apart from your family for hours is hardly the point.

Probably time to repeat this again, but don't abandon your kids, especially to go drinking. What's wrong with you? If your children are old and savvy enough to be on their own, then lay out some time for everyone to go their separate ways. If you are at all sentimental, set regular meeting times. Trust me on this. That first time they go off without you is going to be heartbreaking.

***Disney Drinking Tip.*** When slipping out of a line on an altruistic mission for your family, do not walk directly up to the nearest quick-service counter and grab a beer. Even if you think you are safely beyond the sightlines, your people could spot you by accident. Retreating from the Cozy Cone with two bright yellow cups in your hands is an inconvenient time to discover the group of suddenly observant nighthawks you just left at Mater's Junkyard Jamboree can clearly see you.

# Excuses for Sneaking Off to Get a Drink

Traveling with family, friends, or on one of those fabled Disneyland blind dates? There are times when you just need a moment to yourself. I keep imploring you not to abandon your family. Stepping out for a second, to grab a therapeutic drink, is acceptable if it enables you to return a better person, more energetic, and able to happily face the day. If it truly is a date you're slipping out on, there's likely no future in it. Probably best to just be honest and part ways openly.

What you say will be the determining factor in whether your immediate future involves a glass of wine or a standby queue with your whining brood. I always encourage being truthful, of course. If you have to decide between a number of equal half-truths, keep these suggestions in mind:

*"I will go get FASTPASSES."* This line is positive party-splitting gold. The tradition of sending that responsible member of your group to distant and varied regions of the park predates the FASTPASS by decades. Since the inception of the very first theme park, mothers, husbands, and particularly gullible children have all been put upon to retrieve popcorn, locate specific ice-cream creations, and hold spots on the parade route, while the rest of the family enjoys some amazing roller coaster, some other show, or even just their own selfish lethargy.

At the dawn of amusement, when a prehistoric vacationing family realized they were clear across the park from the one sole lemonade vendor, antediluvian dad would embark upon the vital task of retrieving goods for others, without their thanks or participation. Well, here is where the gofer gets even.

Fast forward to the FASTPASS era. While waiting for Grizzly River Run, that particularly attentive member of your group realizes your window for additional passes is about to open. Everyone wants Soarin' passes pronto, though no one is willing to get out of line. Cue the accountable adult.

At the intersection of Disney California Adventure FASTPASSes and alcoholic beverage availability is where profound opportunity exists for the put-upon theme park provider.

The practice inherently means missing an attraction, and time with your loved ones, but you make up for it with some quality personal space and a neon-bright cup of job well done.

If you go to Disney California Adventure at all, go early and secure Radiator Springs Racers FASTPASSes, first thing. If that fails, shame on you, but it sets up the perfect beer-run opportunity. When your group foolishly decides to ride Radiator Springs via the lamentable standby queue, offer to get FASTPASSes for anything else, even an attraction you do not want to ride. Rather than wait in the Racers standby line, I would offer to go back and sit in the car. Some lines are just a misuse of your time (see Space Mountain and Toy Story Mania).

With your party locked within that positive glacier of a line, embrace the likely hour of freedom stretching out before you. I am loathe to encourage anyone to break off from their family at Disneyland for such a significant block of time. But, if your people aren't keen enough to not squander so many Disney minutes, even for an incredible ride, then I shan't judge or blame you.

*"I forgot something in the car."* This one is a gem, though it requires some serious commitment. There is no such thing as a good parking spot at Disneyland. What can arguably be called the best spots are a country mile from the front gate, and grow logistically more difficult to reach the farther you get into the parks. This excuse is flawless, though you should only use it as a last resort. It will eat up a huge chunk of your Disney day, and you are going to have trouble living with yourself for a while.

The guilt will come from lying to your loved ones, at Disneyland. Because, to make this method work in your favor, you aren't really going all the way back to your car. An actual trip to the parking lot leaves no time for getting or enjoying a drink. So, again, you're going to lie. If you have an ardently developed sense of self-delusion, you don't have think of it as lying, or sneaking off. At this point, you are not being honest with yourself, but you can look at it like you're protecting the feelings of those you care about, by intentionally misleading them.

Your conscience aside, the toughest part of this caper is remembering to hide the thing on your person, which you will later claim to be fetching from the car. It should be concealable, practical, and not something sold at the park. Pretending to go back to the car for a hat, pen, or batteries, will get you an unwanted trip to, and purchase from, the nearest gift shop.

Glasses are a perfect false flag. They work best if you actually wear glasses, and if your family pays little enough attention to you that they won't notice you getting out of the car without them. At the height of desperation, say, when your crew chooses to get in a 40-minute Dumbo line, make your move.

Claim you need to go back to the car. Don't worry about anyone volunteering to accompany you, or go in your stead. If they couldn't be bothered to look out for you in the first place, are they going to do anything so noble now? If you are parked in the Mickey & Friends parking structure, hop the monorail for the most convincing exit with the least amount of walking.

Once out of eyesight, head for the nearest tavern or dispensary of your choice. Pull your glasses out of your secret pocket and read the menu with clear vision, despite your conscience, which will be anything but.

I probably should have mentioned this earlier, but don't pretend to be without your glasses if you truly can't see without them. I applaud desperate measures, but sacrificing any part of your Disneyland visit to blindness is hardly worth that one drink. Except, this maneuver really grants the shameless perpetrator two or three drinks. It's what makes it almost worth all the dishonesty. A trip to the parking lot and back can conceivably take over an hour. Then factor in how your family is surely not going to wait at the monorail station for your return. Reaching a meeting point, then, justifies even more time.

It is essential you do not forget the item you purported to go after. Try to explain to even the most gullible person you know how you managed to fail at the one thing you left to do, and how it still took you an hour to do it. Now, imagine getting through this story without anyone in your incredulous family catching wind of the alcohol on your breath.

*"I need to use the restroom."* While an understandable and regular Disney necessity, if you make this claim, you will most likely wind up with one or all of your children tagging along. Even if

your kids insist they don't need to go, how likely is your partner to let you go off by yourself, leaving them to tend to the entire horde, just so they can handle the joyous restroom gymnastics in five minutes, when it turns out they all have to go desperately?

You also occupy rare real estate if you are anywhere in the park where a restroom is not in view. When you strike off in the exact opposite direction, your party may become suspicious. Then how much time is this ruse going to buy you? Sure, a committed drinker—defined as someone willing to lie to loved ones at Disneyland to spend time away from them—can acquire and drink a beer in the time it takes mere mortals to use the restroom. Does it afford you time to enjoy it, though? And, if use this excuse more than twice, what are you going to say when you really do have to use the bathroom? A suspicious family is one that no longer trusts you to go off on your own.

*"I don't want to go on such-and-such a ride."* This can be a convenient out, or a positive blunder. Depends upon how, where, and when you try to use it, and who else in your party also doesn't favor the attraction in question.

First, it buys you very little time, literally the amount of time it takes your more ambitious family to go on whichever ride you're backing out of. Also, it only works in Disney California Adventure. Sure, you can pretend to not want to go on Splash Mountain, but where does that leave you? In the best of circumstances—which require a completely empty park, except for the Splash Mountain line—you could maybe make it all the way to Award Wieners, touch the window, and run all the way back. That should leave just enough time to compose yourself on the bench where your family left you, as they come out of the attraction. If you noticed, this didn't leave you any time to actually buy or have a drink.

A committed friend of mine suggested Dumbo, a much less enjoyable ride, which is much closer to the front gate. Would be ideal, no? No. That line does, typically, buy one a massive escape window. The problem? Your family does not disappear into a huge artificial mountain at any point. From the line and attraction they would totally see you sprinting off through the castle. Then they would absolutely see you sneaking back.

Disney California Adventure, then, is the place for this little jewel. If you pick your spots properly, it's flawless—unless, of course, you consider dishonesty and hypocrisy to be flaws. That's another matter, surely.

Some of the best escapes were discussed elsewhere, but repetition breeds familiarity. The better acquainted you are, the better your chances of success. As for your chances for domestic tranquility, that depends upon how well you cope with guilt.

Radiator Springs Racers standby line is your hall-of-fame outlet. This standby line is always so long and slow, and such a waste of your time, you needn't even mislead your loved ones about your true intentions. With open honesty and iron resolve, you tell anyone who is willing to stand in this line how doing so is an affront to Walt's memory, and you will not be a party to it.

Radiator Springs Racers is incredible, a can't-miss attraction. If you don't get yourself a FASTPASS early in the day, or if you aren't willing to file into the single-rider line, well, then, I think you're better off missing it. If your family does not agree, let them watch you walk right over to Flo's or the Cozy Cone, and purchase two drinks for yourself. Heck, go over to the Karl Strauss Beer Truck. Return to Flo's outside seating area and grab yourself a table. From the comfort of this peaceful patio, sip delicious beer and watch all the people who wouldn't listen to you as they slog through that life-drainer of a line.

Monsters, Inc. is another perfect candidate, assuming Studio Specialties is open. You can still make it to Award Wieners and back, but Award Wieners doesn't sell margaritas or IPA. A considerable segment of the Monsters. Inc. line winds right next to Studio Specialties. If you claimed you could not ride Monsters, Inc. because you felt sick, needed to sit down, etc., your family can now see you purchasing a large colorful drink, with glow cubes in it, without them. Be sure to have a backup to your fallback story handy.

The Disney Animation pavilion provides an even better escape. It's fully enclosed and Award Wieners is right there. It is, however, a tremendous interactive bonding opportunity for families of any demographic and makeup. Would you seriously run out on your kids first-ever pencil drawing for a beer you don't really like? What's wrong with you?

# CHAPTER SIX

# Disneyland Specialty Cocktails

Have you ever ordered a Hurricane anywhere but New Orleans? In Ireland, can you imagine not drinking whiskey and stout ale? Lazy stereotypes aside, sometimes you have to drift outside your comfort zone to properly experience the unique culture in which you are surrounded. You enjoy Mai Tais, Pina Coladas, and similar tropical drinks, but do you make them at home? Certain beverages just lend themselves to certain locations. Disney is no exception. I can say with confidence, if I ever intentionally order a cocktail with glow cubes in it, it's either going to be on New Year's Eve or at a Disney resort. Probably both.

The Disneyland Resort specialty cocktails menu is designed and presented with as much whimsy as Disney can apply to something so theoretically grown-up. It is compiled in a delightfully bound binder, with illustrations and enticing details of what to expect in and from each individual drink. (Less unique libations are also available, with less fanfare, such as the Ultimate Bloody Mary, Mimosas, Bellinis, and Raspberry Champagne.)

There may be ingredients and combinations with which you are unfamiliar. Disney cast members are masters of their craft, and are unrivaled when it comes to customer service. Feel free to ask questions of your server or bartender. Please try to avoid asking, "What's good?" The cast member before you is likely more patient than I am. They may not even blink when someone they've just met asks for an instant and accurate judgment regarding their personal taste. I always marvel when an adult entrusts a complete stranger to tell them what kind of drink they are likely to enjoy. Probably best I am not in that line of work any longer.

The specialty cocktails menu changes on occasion, though not often and not extensively. To the best of my exhaustive research, the menu is available in its current form at the Cove Bar, Wine Country Trattoria, Hearthstone Lounge, Steakhouse 55, Napa Rose, and each Disney character restaurant: Ariel's Grotto, Goofy's Kitchen, Storytellers Café, and Disney's PCH Grill. Slight theme-driven variations are found at Carthay Circle and Trader Sam's, and some drinks don't appear on all menus. Get to know your server/bartender if you have questions or concerns. At press time, the specialty offerings are:

### Raspberry-Ginger "Vojito"
*Finlandia Raspberry Vodka, Ginger, Mint, Raspberry Purée, and fresh Lime Juice, topped with Coconut Water*

Mojitos have had their day in the sun, and coincidentally that is the best way to enjoy them (see Cove Bar). No offense to the specialty drinks PR people, but it's surprising to see these particular cocktails still on the front page of their menu.

Despite not being cool anymore, this Raspberry-Ginger version is exceptional. The substitution of vodka for rum impresses me. I always prefered vodka, even when making drinks for others. The addition of ginger makes the vojito less sweet than you'd expect.

### Bacardi Mojito
*Bacardi Superior Rum, fresh Lime Juice, Agave Nectar, and Mint, topped with Soda Water*

There is nothing wrong with this drink. I try to resist getting swept up in a trend, and am loath to pretend I never liked a particular something once it's no longer en vogue. Still, I will admit to getting into mojitos a few years back. I hold my friend Vik responsible; specifically, the resort we stayed at in Cabo, for his bachelor party, with the open bar that exclusively served mojitos and a beer I didn't like.

I don't like them anymore. It has mostly to do with how labor intensive they are to make. I no longer tend bar, though my heart goes out to the practitioners of the art who continue to contend with such tedious concoctions. Unless the only other option is a watered-down Mexican lager, order something else.

## Habañero Lime Margarita
*Patrón Silver Tequila, Habañero Lime, and house-made Sweet-and-Sour*

Several problems here, which really should not affect anyone's decision to order this drink. First, I don't like mixing with Patrón. Premium tequila loses its primary value—that glorious bite—when you put juice in it. In order to make your margarita taste like Patrón again, it would have to be so strong you couldn't drink it. At least, so strong you shouldn't be drinking it at Disneyland. Then, if I am going to pay twelve dollars for a margarita, it sure as Panchito isn't going to have sweet-and-sour in it. Thankfully, every Disney bartender I have encountered knows how to make a much more presidential top-shelf margarita. Just ask them.

## Agave Nectar Margarita
*Tres Generaciones Organic Plata Tequila, Agave Nectar, fresh Lime Juice*

This margarita solves every issue I have with the previous offering. No offense to Patrón drinkers, unless you're only into it because of its connection to misogynist pop culture, but Tres Generaciones makes for a consistently better beverage. Agave and lime juice instead of sweet-and-sour, and it's 25 cents cheaper? Order this one.

## Watermelon Margarita
*Patrón Silver Tequila, Watermelon, and fresh Lime Juice*

Here we have the exception to several of the rules I stated above. Removing sweet-and-sour does not automatically resuscitate a questionable margarita recipe. I have tried flavored margaritas with premium tequila, and I do not recommend them, at any price. Unless they're free. There's also a habañero version, but I won't insult either of us by commenting on it.

## Ultimate Long Island Iced Tea
*Bacardi Superior Rum, Tito's Handmade Vodka, Hendrick's Gin, Cointreau, and Sweet-and-Sour with a splash of Coca-Cola*

There are those who maintain mixing several excellent spirits together detracts from each of them. I am one of those people. Rather than have a cocktail with Tito's and Hendrick's in it,

I recommend a cheaper drink that has one or the other. Tito's and Cointreau work well together. It's mixing a premium gin and vodka together, then putting rum in it, to which I object.

If you are irrevocably set on a Long Island, this one is ridiculously good. If you are determined to drink at the Disneyland Resort, I cannot recommend having more than one of these in a 24-hour period.

### Captain's Mai Tai

Captain Morgan Original Spiced Rum, Bols Amaretto, and Tropical Juices, topped with a float of Myers's Original Dark Rum

The Mai Tai is another of those mixed drinks that can sneak up on you. You believe you've ordered an innocuous bucket of fruit juice, then by the time you get to the bottom of it, parts of your body don't obey your brain any longer. Two Mai Tais are acceptable at a destination wedding, if someone else is paying for them. At Disneyland, if children are counting on you to take them on Space Mountain, I recommend zero Mai Tais, though you can probably still function after one.

### Pimm's Punch

Pimm's No. 1 Liqueur, Hendrick's Gin, Odwalla Lemonade, and Wild Strawberry

This is probably not a drink you would select out of a specialty drinks menu because it sounds good to you. The contradiction is, it is really good. You don't know Pimm's? You don't drink gin? This combination will surprise you. True gin drinkers likely wouldn't order one of these. I hesitate to bathe Hendrick's with so many oppressive suspects myself. But, again, I kind of like this mixture. Like I said, though, I'm not a true gin drinker, and those with whom I am familiar would likely soak their fingernails in this as soon as drink it.

### Moscow Mule

*Russian Standard Vodka, fresh Lime Juice, and Agave Nectar, topped with Ginger Beer*

Russian standard vodka has been a personal favorite ever since I was introduced to it by fellow Disney enthusiast and knowledgeable friend, Christine Najac. As mentioned, I am hesitant to mix any liquor I truly like into a bucket of distraction, but the mule concoction works, though $11 seems a little steep for something that isn't terribly labor intensive. It's also difficult to sip something that tastes this wonderful. I suspect Disney has to charge this much to keep you from drinking three of these at lunch.

### Kentucky Mule

*Buffalo Trace Kentucky Straight Bourbon, fresh Lime Juice, and Agave Nectar, topped with Ginger Beer*

I'm not the most committed whiskey or bourbon drinker. I haven't a clue whether this drink works for anyone. I like it okay, though I much prefer the Moscow Mule, and will choose it over this one every time. That's not a slight. It's a personal preference, and I invite everyone to trust their own instincts here. Understand that Fireball is my primary inlet to any type of whiskey. I wholly admit to being a poor judge on the matter.

### Piña Colava

*Bacardi Raspberry Rum with Piña Colada mix and Raspberry Purée*

This is a delicious drink. It's also really, really sweet. I can get about two ounces down before I start looking for the bowl of spicy snack mix. If this type of beverage appeals to you, I suggest you make your way to Trader Sam's and order a Piranha Pool. It's no less of a popsicle, but it does have vodka instead of rum, and comes surrounded by incomparable Trader Sam's charm.

### Bahama Mama

*Parrot Bay Coconut Rum, Myers's Original Dark Rum, Bols Crème de Banana, and Tropical Juices*

You either like banana-flavored drinks, or you do not. I love Bananas Foster, the dessert. That love does not translate to an affinity for this seemingly similar cocktail. There's something that just doesn't work here for me. And I don't think it's the coconut, because I love coconut. It's not even the idea of a banana drink. Pretty much every smoothie I make, drink, and enjoy has banana in it. I don't know how this mystery will ever get solved either, as I don't forsee experimenting with this particular drink ever again.

### Smoked Turkey

*Wild Turkey 101 Bourbon, Red Stag Black Cherry Bourbon, Grenadine, and Odwalla Lemonade with a hint of Hickory Smoke, garnished with Luxardo Gourmet Maraschino Cherries*

I am no bourbon expert. I don't want to push any unwitting novice into a regrettable decision, any more than I would like to steer a committed bourbon drinker away from something they might enjoy. This cocktail sounds like something I would be afraid to spill on my shoes. I suspect, if I start drinking one, that's precisely what would happen.

### Rye Manhattan

*Bulleit Rye Small Batch American Whiskey, Carpano Antica Sweet Vermouth, and Angostura Bitters, garnished with Luxardo Gourmet Maraschino Cherries*

At the risk of angering bourbon and whiskey purists, this looks a lot like the Smoked Turkey. At any rate, both drinks fall outside my purview. I have had Bulleit, and like it. I don't think I would like it in Manhattan form. If you like Manhattans, though, I am prepared to accept that this is a good one. I will leave it to the experts.

### Blue "Glow-tini"

*SKYY Infusions Citrus Vodka, Peach Schnapps, Blue Curaçao, and Pineapple Juice, with a sugared rim and a souvenir Glow Cube*

As I mentioned, if I am going to drink a cocktail with glow cubes in it, you better believe I am going to do it at a Disney resort. I also guarantee it won't be this one. SKYY has done a masterful job with their flavored vodkas. I am partial to SKYY as I maintain it is the secret ingredient in Fillmore's Pomegranate Limeade.

However, citrus vodka, peach schnapps, and blue curaçao is a combination I would expect to encounter in a bathtub at a freshman dorm. Were I to drink any of it, someone better hold my hair back, because it's headed for the commode.

### Magical Star Cocktail

*X-Fusion Organic Mango and Passion Fruit Liqueur, Parrot Bay Coconut Rum, Pineapple Juice, and a souvenir multi-colored Glow Cube*

Here we have a more palatable mix, and an even more glori-ously tinted cocktail. It is fortunate, and I can say this about half of Disney's specialty cocktails, that you can't drink this prior to boarding the Tea Cups. With such a combination of sweetness, disparate juices, and liqueurs, rapid movement is a dangerous ingredient to add to this recipe.

## Sidecar Noir

*Fireball Cinnamon Whiskey, Cointreau Noir, Orange Juice, and fresh Lime Juice*

I am familiar with Fireball whiskey. It's why I'm comfortable cautioning everyone to avoid the Sidecar Noir as if it had a toenail in it. Even if its flavor combination sounds like something you might enjoy, I recommend you try anything else. Don't think the debilitating nature of this drink is tempered by the presence of Cointreau. Cointreau Noir is not the whimsical orange liqueur you pour into your margaritas when you're purging your friend's bar and can't find Grand Marnier. Cointreau Noir is basically Cognac. So, someone thought it would be clever to mix Fireball—everyone's favorite party killer—with another undrinkable, unpredictable liquor. It might be entertaining to witness the ruin of someone trying to put a couple of these down at a private party. At Disneyland, you'd be better off with a Jägermeister Boilermaker (don't drink that either).

## Fireball Cocktail

*Fireball Cinnamon Whiskey and RumChata Cream Liqueur*

If my admonition above, and this monstrosity's ingredients don't ward you off, I don't know what to tell you. Please don't sit anywhere near me on any of the roller-coaster-style attractions.

## Godiva Chocolate Martini

*Godiva Chocolate Liqueur, Stoli Vanil Vodka, Bols White Crème de Cacao, and Frangelico*

Here we have the Long Island Iced Tea of dessert drinks, with four types of alcohol, all of which taste like candy. And like the Long Island, this beauty will go straight to your head and leave you wondering why you are so sleepy all of a sudden. It doesn't sound like it, with all the chocolate, cream, and vanilla, but we are fortunate this one has enough of a bite to keep you from slamming it. If it also keeps you from ordering a second one after dinner, perhaps you can make it back to the park.

### Banana-spiced Rum Martini

*Captain Morgan Original Spiced Rum, Bols Crème de Banana, Cream Liqueur*

Once my favorite brand of alcohol, were I to now consume Captain Morgan, delivered in this manner, it would likely be for the last time. Banana spice would make an intriguing flavor of hard candy. I might even try one if it came in stick form at the Candy Palace on Main Street. As a booze-heavy beverage, it would affect me the way Mad Tea Party wrecks people who ride it when they don't really want to.

### Red Sangria

*Beso Del Sol Red made from a 100% natural marriage of Spanish Tempranillo Grapes, Orange, Blood Orange, and Lemon Juices, with a touch of natural Cinnamon*

Do you like sangria? If so, you will love Disney's red sangria. The wine, juice, fruit, and spices they use are all wonderfully suited for a sangria mixture. Its current price of $9.50 is a steep one to pay to test if you like something, but if you are even curious about such a drink, you will probably enjoy it.

### White Sangria

*Beso Del Sol White made from a 100% natural blend of Airén White Spanish Grapes, Peach, and Mango Juices*

White sangria is more of an acquired-taste cocktail. Red wine sangria typically blends into a refreshing punch. Many white wines possess a sweetness that makes mixing them in this fashion a little dicey. Sweeter than punch, even, white sangria resembles a glass of melted popsicles. Delicious, sure, but how much popsicle can you drink without intestinal discomfort?

## *Beer Selection (all 12oz bottles)*

- Sierra Nevada Pale Ale (Chico)
- Firestone Walker Double Barrel Ale (Paso Robles)
- Boulevard Pop-Up Session IPA (Kansas City)
- Figueroa Mountain Hoppy Poppy IPA (Santa Ynez Valley)
- Bear Republic Racer 5 IPA (Healdsburg)
- Napa Smith Hopageddon Imperial IPA (Napa)
- Karl Strauss Tower 10 IPA (San Diego)
- Hangar 24 Orange Wheat Ale (Redlands)

- Anaheim Hefeweizen (Anaheim)
- Blue Moon Belgian White (Golden, CO)
- North Coast Pranqster Belgian (Fort Bragg)
- New Belgium Fat Tire (Ft. Collins, CO)

A dedicated California based entity, the loyalty Disneyland demonstrates toward local commodities and artistic elements makes one proud to be a fellow native. Of course, Starbucks exercises its unavoidable influence, and Budweiser products appear on most every menu, but people the world over favor, and come to expect, such familiar luxuries. Disney is not going to alienate guests, just to appear hip to the capricious minority.

All around the resort, and inside Disney California Adventure specifically, guests are introduced to and embraced by stellar examples of native Californian fare and beverages.

If that's not your thing, they also have the typical array of bottled beer: Budweiser, Bud Light, Coors Light, Corona Extra, Dos Equis, Heineken, Miller Lite, and Stella Artois

## The Disney Family of Wines

Who hasn't dreamed of working for Disney? Ever since I knew that was a thing that regular people were able to do, I wanted to be a Disneyland cast member. Growing up, my bucket-list Disney jobs were Jungle Cruise skipper, Matterhorn mountain climber, and Pirates of the Caribbean ride operator. I wanted to wear a pirate costume to work even before I ever thought about working for Disney. Truth is, I still want to. Had I realized there were people inside the character costumes, it would have broken my heart, but I would have then wanted to be Donald Duck. Donald was always my favorite.

Through an unbelievable confluence of circumstances a few years back, I did manage to get a job as a Disneyland Hotel banquet bartender. There was nothing pirate-like about the uniform, but Mickey Mouse himself handed me my name tag on my first day. So, needless to say, dreams come true.

Years later, I still want to skipper the Jungle Cruise. And I'm a little more apprehensive, but would probably climb the Matterhorn given the opportunity, in lederhosen, of course. My most recent, enthusiastic dream is more about having my books appear in Disneyland gift shops. Okay, what I really want is for them to appear right next to the park guide maps at the front gate. Ideally, I'm looking for Disney to purchase pallets of them and give them out for free, with the maps. However, I don't know how that would affect my Amazon bestseller status.

Even celebrities dream of being part of the Disney cast. Rumor has it Robin Williams and Wayne Brady once worked in the Magic Kingdom, and, as huge stars, both returned for regular park appearances, movies, television, and voice work.

Now, wine people have their own professional and social circles, and their own opinions on what is cool, or impressive. Even the largest California vintner, I imagine, would love to have their label appear at a Disney resort. To be welcome into the Disney Family of Wines has to be similarly wonderful.

The Disney Family of Wines is an exclusive group of fine California vineyards, appearing throughout Disney California Adventure and throughout the specialty drinks menu. As you make your way around the Disneyland Resort, those of a mind to notice such things may observe certain consistently available items in the restaurants, gift shops, coffee carts, and, indeed, the bars. Close readers of this guide will presume Karl Strauss Tower 10 IPA is sold everywhere. It should be, though it really only seems like it here, because I keep mentioning it.

Independent of my bias, but with my full enthusiasm, California breweries are the predominant purveyors of beer at the resort, and not simply within Disney California Adventure. Downtown Disney and the hotels stock a hearty variety of native labels. Steakhouse 55 had Karl Strauss Aurora Hoppyalis and Ballast Point Sculpin on tap at the same time for a couple weeks. I almost applied for a job, until it occurred to me, working at a well-managed bar is an effective means of ensuring you won't be able to drink there.

Disney also demonstrates a decided loyalty toward certain wine labels. Again, those with a mind and eye for it have gotten to know Lasseter, MacMurray Ranch, and Silverado through the years. These prestigious California vineyards independently made their mark on the outside world. Now, brought together by a shared connection to Disney, each belong to an exclusive, rather remarkable family.

From true family ties—Silverado Vineyards was founded by Walt's daughter, Diane—to unshakable sentimental bonds—Fred MacMurray, Fess Parker, and Kurt Russell are Disney film and television legends—Disney's historical landscape is in part defined by the strata formed by the eight privileged members of this exclusive family of wines

In toto, the family—Silverado Vineyards, Fess Parker Winery, MacMurray Estate Vineyards, Lasseter Family Winery, Gogi Wines, Frank Family Vineyards, Chappellet Winery, and Skywalker Vineyards—may be found, sampled, and enjoyed at the glorious Alfresco Tasting Terrace. You can also find each, in reduced and variable combinations, throughout the resort.

There are many other, and, I'll say it, better wines sold all around the resort. But the family connection is charming. At press time, these Disney Family Wines were available:

## Silverado Vineyards

Cofounded by Diane Disney Miller, daughter of Walt and Lillian Disney. That qualifies as family. Upon learning of her involvement, Silverado became my go-to wine at the resort, and given the choice, at a grocery store.

- Savignon Blanc, Napa Valley
- Cardonnay, Carneros
- Merlot, Napa Valley
- Fantasia, Napa Valley
- Cabernet Sauvignon, Napa Valley

## Fess Parker Winery

Founded by Disney's original, undeniable Davy Crockett.

- Syrah, Santa Barbara County
- Pinot Noir, Santa Barbara County

## MacMurray Estate Vineyards

Founded by the absent-minded professor himself, Fred MacMurray.

- Pinot Gris, Sonoma
- Pinot Noir, Russian River Valley

## Lasseter Family Winery

Owned by Pixar CCO, and former Jungle Cruise Skipper, John Lasseter. I still have it in mind to pilot a Jungle Cruise one day. As a cast member, I mean. Don't volunteer your services as a guest. The cast members won't think it's a good idea, nor will the boat full of strangers who didn't come to see you spiel.

- Rosé, Sonoma Valley
- Malbec, Sonoma Valley

## Gogi Wines

Owned by Kurt Russell, who has starred in more television and motion picture productions for Walt Disney Studios than any other human.

- Chardonnay, Santa Barbara County
- Pinot Noir, Lompoc

## Frank Family Vineyards

Richard H. Frank served as president of the Walt Disney Studios for a decade, beginning in the mid-1980s, and as chairman of Walt Disney Television. I would say that kind of resume warrants serving your wine at Napa Rose.

- Chardonnay, Napa Valley
- Cabernet Sauvignon, Napa Valley

## Chappellet Winery

Frank Wells, president and CEO of The Walt Disney Company for ten years, married into the Napa Chappellet family.

- Cuvee, Napa Valley
- Zinfandel, Napa Valley

## Skywalker Vineyards

George Lucas' winery, clearly. Lucas lost his mind with Jar Jar Binks. For the overwhelmingly positive contribution the Star Wars brand has made to Disneyland, Walt Disney World, and runDisney, I shall not pan the man's wine nor question its place within the Disney family.

- Pinot Noir, Marin County

CHAPTER SEVEN

# The Best of
# Drinking at Disneyland

The rankings for this particular section are entirely subjective and admittedly don't take personal drinking preferences into account. If you don't like outside seating, or only drink wine, first, broaden your horizons a little. Second, understand the following list details seven spots around the Disneyland Resort where you ought to just take a minute, take a seat, and enjoy the sensation of not running yourself ragged, if only for a moment.

The Disneyland Resort pools are not included in this list, as they are meant for the exclusive use of Disneyland Resort hotel guests. This list is intended for the enjoyment of all guests. The Disneyland Hotel and Grand Californian pools would rank first and second, otherwise.

## Club 33, New Orleans Square, Disneyland

If you are able to get yourself in a position to even wash your hands in a Club 33 lavatory, count yourself among the truly blessed. If you have the type of access whereby you can sit and have a drink inside Club 33, well, yeah, I recommend it.

## Mendocino Tasting Terrace,
## Pacific Wharf, Disney California Adventure

On a sunny day, or within hours of a parade, you will have trouble finding a table here. If so, head up the expanse of stairs on the left and see if the Alfresco Terrace is open. Alfresco is a little more secluded, without quite the advantageous people watching, or it would be on this list by itself. The hours of operation are also a little difficult to predict. With a glass of wine in your hand, a seat at Mendocino, it's easy to forget where you are and what you thought you were supposed to be doing. Another glass, and you won't care.

## Carthay Circle Lounge, Buena Vista Street, Disney California Adventure

Perhaps Disney's concession to all who cannot get into Club 33, Carthay is a beautiful demonstration of Disney design and creativity. It doesn't have Club 33's history, though it is rich with layers of Disney-fashioned authenticity. Transport back to a clean, safe version of a point in our past that was neither. No one delivers imagination like Disney, even in what is essentially a glorified waiting area.

## Trader Sam's, Disneyland Hotel

It's kitschy, it's crowded, and it's about as far from the Matterhorn as you can get. It is also an extraordinary example of what a handful of creative Disney minds are capable. As much attraction as restaurant, you must see the place at least once. If you can find a seat inside, take it. The patio and cushioned seating outside is not a lamentable downgrade, and will still make the trip down here worthwhile.

## Tortilla Jo's, Downtown Disney District

The restaurant is muy bueno, the taqueria is exceptionally convenient, but for the purposes of this list we direct you to the Cantina. Partial to a delightful patio, obviously, I am also a huge fan of anywhere I can get chips, salsa, fresh air, and a salt-rimmed cocktail.

## Catal Lounge, Downtown Disney District

Beautiful, comfortable, if you've got a minute to spend in luxury, come find it at Catal. I would recommend the Timon parking lot if they had couches and Karl Strauss IPA. It doesn't. This second-story lounge does, and it also has TVs on one wall and a terrific view out the other. It's also a full bar. You don't have to have beer unless you want to, and unless they are still pouring Aurora Hoppyalis.

## Splitsville, Downtown Disney District

It's not open yet, or would appear higher on this list. I've been to the one at Walt Disney World. I love it, and have complete faith the new one will be similarly spectacular. It's why it appears on this list at all. The patio bar I expect them to build will mirror Tortilla Jo's cantina, geographically, should rival it, and is going to mean a much-needed increase in glorious outdoor seating.

# Top Disney Drinks and Where Best to Enjoy Them

Do you know why a Coke purchased from the Main Street Refreshment Corner tastes better than any other Coke you can get anywhere else in the world? It's the same reason every Disney park or resort purchase is the best, most satisfying example of its type. Because you are surrounded by acres and hours of Disney-dedicated brilliance.

Everything within the confines of a Disney property, from the popcorn you can't resist, to the people you encounter, to the very air you breathe, is just simply better. Oftentimes, what you acquire is even further enhanced by exactly where you got it and how you enjoyed it. Ice cream from Main Street is better than ice cream from Downtown Disney. No offense to the latter. You just can't compete with certain environs, traditions, views, smells, and atmospheric music.

Locate the following beverages, then seek out the precise location described for the ideal enjoyment of each. Like a well-conceived wine and cheese pairing, the extra step adds layers of inarguable bliss.

## Fillmore's Pomegranate Limeade while exploring Cars Land

To enter Cars Land is to be transported directly into the imagination of Disney's most creative minds. Modeled after and replicated exactly like *Cars* the movie, it is as close as you can get to actually living in a cartoon. Where ToonTown creates a sense of heightened anxiety, Cars Land infuses guests with a dreamlike inner peace.

This exact sensation may be captured in your taste buds with the assistance of Fillmore's Pomegranate Limeade. It is stand-alone amazing. Disney could sell it in the parking structure and it would still have made this list. This exquisite elixir is exclusively available at the Cozy Cone Motel dining area. Relatively tucked away, these quick-service concessions do a consistent, bustling business—certainly more than the few tables can accommodate. And that's a blessing, as it compels one to take their delicious fruity wonder, topped with a whipped citrusy taste explosion, and explore the surrounding creativity.

Grab a limeade for each member of your party as they are impossible to share in a manner that will satisfy anyone. Cruise over to Mater's Junkyard Jamboree next door, and chortle at the clever voiceover. Stroll past the former site of Luigi's Flying Tires and reminisce about this timeless, under-appreciated attraction. Perhaps the best use of your time and delightful drink awaits at Radiator Springs Racers. The popularity of this relatively new ride shows no signs of abating, nor does the standby wait time. You are allowed to take these family-friendly beverages with you in line, and as sadly-slow as this one moves, you will be glad you did.

## Wildberry Lemonade within the Carthay Circle Lounge

There are two elements that should eliminate a drink like this from consideration. First, it's really sweet. Outside of a well-made margarita, I don't like mixed drinks much myself. Between Fillmore's and this Wildberry concoction, it's like I don't even know myself anymore.

Second, it's non-alcoholic. WHAT? Seriously, throw this entire book in the trash. No, don't really do that. Hear me out at least....

If you can catch a Carthay server and bartender who isn't overwhelmed—not a simple matter in this exceedingly popular venue—a Wildberry Lemonade Cocktail has the potential to become your favorite anything. Disney cast members are used to going that extra mile, and requesting one doctor a non-alcoholic specialty beverage is certainly not asking for the world. They will do it, even when they're busy. When they're not, your drink will receive the attention it and you deserve, and that's when the true magic happens.

In the days and months I have been singing the praises of this drink, my detractors have wondered, "Rather than go to all the trouble, why wouldn't I just order something simpler, that I know I like already." Okay, you can do that. A vodka cranberry is a reasonable drink. It's reliable, and won't stump or anger any Disney bartender. Your mundane drink is also the weak, watered-down second cousin of Wildberry Lemonade. They're as different as "it's a small world" and Pirates of the Caribbean. Vodka-Cran tastes like it comes from one of those foil-lined pouches you have to puncture with a pokey straw. Whereas, Wildberry Lemonade, you don't taste it so much as it passes from your lips into your soul, to the accompaniment of violin music and a neck massage.

If your order isn't complicated enough already, you still have to straighten out how you want alcohol in this complete hassle of a beverage. Be you a vodka or a gin drinker, requesting your favorite of either is going to cement the Wildberry Lemonade in your cocktail Hall of Fame. I suggest you don't go overly premium with the liquor. Belvedere Vodka is wonderful, but it's going to disappear in a drink like this. As will Hendrick's Gin. You won't realize the true grown-up splendor of this whole endeavor until you try to stand up. Tito's and Tanqueray, respectively, each create a divine Wildberry Lemonade Cocktail.

The reason it's a hassle at all, is the reason you want it most. Wildberry Lemonade comes topped with a fruit foam you will want to bathe in. Topped, that is, within the restaurant kitchen. Therein lies the rub. Wildberry Lemonade has to be specially prepared in the kitchen, and then you are asking the lounge staff to augment it. Again, you are not asking the bartender to donate bone marrow, but I am someone who disliked receiving orders for Guinness when I was busy, because it takes so long to pour.

You are completely within your rights to order a drink the way you want it. If you share my sense of empathy, what you can do is order a straight Wildberry Lemonade, and a shot of gin or vodka. Then mix it yourself. It's a little more expensive to do it this way. The barkeep will appreciate it, and you, even if they don't truly realize the service you have rendered them.

## Agave Nectar Margarita at the Cove Bar

There's almost always a line to get a seat in the Cove Bar. It usually rivals that of Toy Story Midway Mania. If you can get in, and you get a primo margarita, the time and energy you sacrifice will be worth it.

At a table by the rail—again, if there's one available— enjoying a margarita in the sunshine, is about the best way to spend any moment of your Disney visit that does not involve rides and eating. The people watching is splendid, though if the sounds of screaming from the neighboring roller coaster don't inhibit it, you cannot be faulted for simply staring blankly at the lagoon, as you slip into a near-hypnotic trance.

An Agave Nectar Margarita is cabeza and shoulders above any other margarita on the specialty drinks menu. It may not be like any margarita with which you are familiar, and I am loathe to recommend anything that would detract from what is supposed to be a top ten Disney drinking experience. The line alone may have done that. Cove Bar bartenders are all well able to make a more recognizable top-shelf Margarita. It will be incredible, and will also facilitate a welcome mid-afternoon oblivion.

## Karl Strauss Tower 10 IPA, sitting out on Pacific Wharf

Blessedly, there are a number of wonderful locations to find Karl Strauss throughout the Disneyland Resort. Hearthstone Lounge and Uva standout like rose bushes in this vast, bountiful garden. I cannot, however, recommend anywhere outside the parks over any place inside the parks.

The Pacific Wharf Distribution Co. is your interior-park home for the glory that is Karl Strauss handcrafted beer. There's often a line. It fits that the more you crave a beer, the longer the line is apt to be. Each tend to be fairly dependent upon the day's attendance. If you care about craft beer in a manner befitting a worthwhile human being, you can endure the line.

Grabbing a margarita or cerveza at one of the neighboring quick-service counters, which have less of a line, will help.

Pretend I didn't just recommend you get a drink to bide the time while waiting for a drink at a family theme park. The Karl Strauss line is a doozy, but you can probably survive it without a crutch beer. If there are children, friends, and spouses waiting for you somewhere, do it for them.

If you truly can't wait, the nearest Karl Strauss is available at the Cove Bar. If Pacific Wharf has a line you can't tolerate, Cove Bar is going to be downright repellent. When one is bad, the other is obscene. If you want to hustle over to Bayside Brews, the payoff is usually worth the extra effort and distance.

Whether you weather the line or not, make your way back to the wharf to drink your beer. Locate a table on the rail. Post up beside the simulated harbor, and let a full-flavored brew speed your transition back to turn-of-the-twentieth-century, sun-dappled San Francisco.

## Dole Whip Float with Rum, sneaking into the Disneyland Hotel pool

Were Disneyland hotel pools open to the general public, it would spoil the tranquility, like that scene from *Caddyshack*. If we could get in, without the requirement of staying at the hotel, and somehow not overwhelm the tiny slice of paradise, the pools would account for eight of the ten locations on this list.

As it is, I can't advise anyone not staying at a Disneyland hotel to violate Disney policy. They aren't militant about all of the rules, but cross the wrong line and you risk losing some rather dear park privileges. I don't wish that upon anyone.

I do urge everyone to locate the Disneyland Hotel's Coffee House. For reasons not well delineated, the Coffee House now sells the coveted Dole Whip. If you are of age, you can get it with rum. If you're staying at the Disneyland Hotel, you can take it over to the pool and enjoy the type of exclusive privilege that you absolutely have to hold over the heads of your social media friends.

For decades, Disney exhibited no demonstrable urgency to make this extremely popular signature treat more widely available. You couldn't even find it beyond its sole congested concession stand inside Adventureland. Like a ticket to a Beyoncé concert, Dole Whip popularity vastly outpaced the practicality of acquiring one. The eternal Tiki Juice Bar line often rivaled that of Peter Pan's Flight, even on cold and rainy days.

At any time of day, or year, in any kind of weather, the craving for wholly wonderful pineapple soft serve is undeniable. Rare is the occasion when guests aren't rendering impassable one of Disneyland's more vital pedestrian thoroughfares. In an unfortunate and rare display of poor spatial management, Adventureland is a virtual pinch point and houses one of the resort's more popular restrooms.

There is a way to acquire Disneyland's most coveted refreshment, without the prolonged wait. It is becoming an ever loosely held insider tip, to the chagrin of those who once thought we were on to something. There is a way around that inexorable throng stretching off toward the Jungle Cruise.

If you can duck through the crowd and get to the Enchanted Tiki Room waiting area, there is another Tiki Juice Bar counter in the courtyard. It is open a lot more often now, as more guests discover its blessed existence. There's usually a line here, too, as word continues to leak out. Yet, it is always shorter, and you aren't out in the press of the walkway. There's also the added entertainment of animatronic Tiki totems and pyrotechnics.

Walt Disney World first, finally, broke the Dole Whip seal. A couple years back they brought the vanilla-pineapple delicacy outside of the Magic Kingdom and over to the aptly themed Polynesian Village Resort. Pouring salt in the wounds of Disneyland guests, the Polynesian then started selling several versions of the Dole Whip Float with rum in it.

Flash forward to today, to the Disneyland Resort. Okay, it's at an obscure hotel coffee shop, but it's the same delicious Dole Whip you know and love. Better, they've got the one with rum. Even better, you can take it to the incredible Disneyland Hotel pool. (Hotel guests only, right? Wink, wink.)

## Wine at a wine terrace

I am hard pressed to select and recommend any specific wine, as wine tastes and preferences are so diverse. Truth be told, the difficulty lies in my profound, implacable partiality toward

IPA. In the interest of capturing more diverse interests, I want to at least steer interested visitors to sample the wonderful wares of Disney California Adventure's Golden Vine Winery, even if I do it so rarely myself.

White, red, rosé, sparkling, and about a hundred labels to choose from, there will be a glass of something on at least one of the terraces to impress all but the most insufferable wine snob. If you don't like wine at all, let the sommelier cast members pour you tasters until something clicks. No one with an open mind hates all kinds of wine.

When you find the one that suits you, or better, if you spot a sentimental favorite on the list, take it to a table on the veranda, and enjoy what may be the first bit of relaxation you've allowed yourself this whole trip. Disneyland is extraordinary, but it's not inherently peaceful. No fault to anyone who fills every moment with rides, railroads, parades, popcorn, FASTPASSes, photo ops, Jedis, jelly beans, and mountains full of roller coasters. Time simply evaporates within a Disney park. The compulsion to try to do everything is almost subconscious.

Therein lies the blessing of the wine terraces, the patios, the wharf, of every emblematic green park bench. If you can, any time you can, find a spot with some partial shade and reflect upon the wonder that surrounds you. If you're keen enough to do it at all, chances are you thought to get a glass of wine first, whereby you are the envy of those with less foresight.

## Scottish Raspberry Lemon Drop in the lobby of Disney's Grand Californian

There is something about Disneyland that piques my desire for sweet, exotic cocktails. I would never order, and certainly wouldn't try to make, anything like this at home. Fillmore's Limeade, Wildberry such-and-such, drinks I don't consider anywhere else, I positively seek out at a Disney park. Like yellow popcorn, and only walking through the left-hand tunnel when I enter Disneyland, certain elements are now just an inseparable part of the experience.

The exquisite taste and creativity ingrained in this gin, raspberry, and agave cocktail is now forever connected to Disney's

Grand Californian awe-inspiring property. Specifically the lobby, where I most often enjoy it, sparks and harnesses my desire for a frothy gin cocktail. Every seat around the edge of the lobby, facing inward, works perfectly for this endeavor. If you're in one of these seats, and someone stands over you with a slight air of impatience, it's probably me, and it's probably because the rest of the seats are taken.

# CHAPTER EIGHT

# Disneyland Drinking Quick Reference

Disneyland does not serve alcohol. This fact is well known and rather widely lamented. Still, many, mostly infrequent visitors are unaware that the sprawling resort surrounding the original park is brimming with adult beverage options. Some guests go from the parking lot, to the park, and back, only venturing outside the gate to catch the tram back to the parking lot. They visit so seldom, they can't justify park hopping, and understanding Disneyland to be a dry campus, they never think to explore Downtown Disney for adult refreshment.

Sound familiar? Your ignorance and forbearance is unfortunate, but curable. From anywhere in the resort, you are mere steps away from adult refreshment. Sure, if you're in Toontown you may as well be in the Kalahari, but it's your fault for venturing all the way back there. Even from Toontown, a train, monorail, or some committed speed walking will shortly have you in more accommodating confines, enjoying an adult beverage of your choice.

Here are some tips, tricks, and quick routes to sanctuary and salvation.

## From Inside Disneyland

*Mickey's Toontown.* We'll start here, as it's about as far as you can get, geographically and psychologically, from grown up refreshment and contentment (also applies to "it's a small world").

Whether in search of a drink, or simply beating a hasty retreat from the surrounding chaos, the first order of business is to get out of there. Easier said than done. Toontown's exit can prove elusive, and there is likely a George R. R. Martin novel's worth of warring families between you and it. DO NOT strike out in a panic. It's the surest way to get pulled deeper into the mayhem.

Keep your wits about you. Stand firm. If you can make any sense at all of the crowd about you, try to turn so you are facing upstream. Close your eyes and hold out your arms. What you're going for here is something akin to that scene in *Unbreakable*, with Bruce Willis in the train station.

As people brush past you, reach out with your conscious mind. Sift through the resignation, while remaining aware for anyone with an overt sense of purpose. Seek out that person, with a spark within them that says, "I am done with this." Latch onto them, your savior, even if you have to grab them physically. Follow them to the Promised Land, and if you truly did grab a stranger, you should explain why. They will empathize with your urgency, and will likely join you for a drink.

Once beyond the Toontown tunnel, an adult beverage is within reach, though you now have an important decision to make. Critical factors include how crowded the park is that day, and the state of your feet. In a vacuum, the most pleasurable option is to head right up to the Toontown railroad station. There you take the train to Main Street, and exit the park. If you have a park hopper, I recommend you then go into Disney California Adventure.

Carthay Circle is your best, closest park hopping option, though this depends, again, upon that day's park attendance. With a crowd, the Carthay Lounge can be a difficult place to get a drink, a table, or even a foot in the door. If so, Smokejumpers Grill becomes the go-to. An argument may be made for Award Wieners, as it is technically closer to the front gate. Remember, though, Award Wieners only offers one beer, and doesn't open until 11:00 am. Smokejumpers is the first of these three to open, at 10:30am. I don't know how early they start pouring beer. They may well do it right when they open, but I'm not saying they won't judge you for ordering one.

If your Toontown experience is such that you can't wait until 10:30, or if you can't go/aren't going into Disney

California Adventure this day, La Brea Bakery Cafe has you covered. La Brea opens at 8:00am. You have to go into the restaurant proper to get alcohol. If you've B-lined here from Toontown, though, are you really going to object to a seat and some table service?

*Critter Country.* This is another unfortunate location to discover yourself in the grips of alcohol withdrawal. Regardless of preference and time pressure, there will be walking in your future. For the shortest walk, head straight for the New Orleans Square railroad station, even though you then face a lengthy train ride, and a potentially long wait.

To break up the journey, without adding to the walk considerably, get off the train in Tomorrowland, and skip over to the monorail. Ride into Downtown Disney and take your pick of festive, fulfilling alternatives. For a quick, close, and delightful respite, do not overlook Earl of Sandwich. There's no bar, but there's also none of the wait and chaos you can expect at the nearby themed restaurants.

Earl of Sandwich boasts a couple beers, a few types of wine, and wide-open seating for the weary. I shouldn't say there's no wait. The place is quite popular. If you're not eating, and you're polite about it, sometimes those in the queue will let you slip in and grab a beverage, without the necessity of waiting in the entire line. I do not recommend this approach. Getting in the back of the line will give you time to browse the menu, until you change your mind and decide to get a sandwich after all.

Nothing wrong with coming to Earl of Sandwich just for beer; not in my opinion, anyway. If you can pass through the restaurant, then sit on the patio watching everyone else eat artfully assembled delicacies, without getting one yourself, you have an unnecessary amount of poorly directed willpower.

*Tomorrowland.* Except for being at or near Disneyland's front gate, Tomorrowland provides the most convenient escape for desperate drinkers. If the park is not terribly crowded, and your sense of urgency outweighs any foot discomfort, you need only walk down Main Street, out of the park, then either to Carthay Circle, if you are park hopping, or into the welcoming arms of Downtown Disney, if you are not.

If walking sounds uninviting, hop on the Disneyland Railroad or the monorail. The train is one stop from Main Street. From there, you are free to pursue Disney California Adventure and Downtown Disney options. The monorail is a quick, pleasurable means to get to the heart of Downtown Disney. ESPN Zone and Rainforest Café are immediately adjacent to the station. Neither is likely to produce rapid refreshment or relaxation, but both are wonderful if you are in the market for what they're offering.

Readers of this book are likely looking for something less hectic, with less required to get an actual drink in hand. I direct you, then, to Tortilla Jo's. The quick service taqueria is ideal for those in desperate need. With several beer options, a choice of frozen margaritas, and almost no waiting...if you are aware of it, you would probably rather I shut up about it. Tortilla Jo's cantina is another excellent option if you're hankering for a stronger drink, an extra level of service, and free chips.

# From Inside Disney California Adventure

No one needs direction and access to an immediate cocktail more desperately than the poor slob marooned on an "it's a small world" watercraft. And Disney drinking veterans will question the necessity for a separate section of directions for guests within Disney California Adventure itself. To you I ask, do you remember your first visit, making your own series of, understandable, rookie mistakes? Did you wait an entire hour for Midway Mania? Did you go on Grizzly River Run thinking there was even a chance you wouldn't get wet? Did you do the tortilla factory tour? Tell me you wouldn't have traded your park ticket for a quick drink in any of those situations.

*Buena Vista Street.* We have described several times how, from anywhere near Disney California Adventure's front gate, you have three theoretically immediate beverage options. If you opt for Carthay Circle, your drink won't be quick, specifically, but geographically it's close. Award Wieners, also nearby, is quick and worthwhile, as long as you aren't too choosy.

Smokejumpers has a few more beers options. One of them is currently a Karl Strauss IPA. Go there, period.

*Hollywood Land.* If Studio Specialties is open, and that's a significant if, it's a handy place to grab a drink in the backlot. If not, you've got Award Wieners and its lone beer, or Carthay and potentially excessive waiting. Careful planning will keep you from venturing into this corner of the park without a preliminary drink in hand, or other recourse.

*"a bug's land".* Disney California Adventure's dry county. It's primarily designed for and populated by young children, so I'm okay with having to go elsewhere to procure alcohol. Most of the ways out lead straight to IPA, Fillmore's Pomegranate Limeade, and wine terrace paradise. If you mistakenly head in the wrong direction, it'll mean a lengthy walk through Hollywood Land, with one-beer-wonder Award Wieners waiting to provide marginal relief. It can happen to anyone (me, for instance). Learn from your mistakes. More important, learn how to locate the wine terraces from wherever you find yourself.

*Cars Land and Pacific Wharf.* Congratulations. You have reached the Promised Land. To find refreshment, you need only get in line. Any line. I recommend the Karl Strauss beer truck, Fillmore's Pomegranate Limeade, Medocino, and Alfresco Tasting Terrace. Not all at once. There are people, mostly children, everywhere, trying to hang on to their youthful innocence.

*Paradise Pier.* Another beating heart of adult beverage satisfaction. Paradise Pier can be the easiest, most pleasurable place to get a drink, depending upon the state of the Cove Bar. When you can't get in there, it can be a trek for alternatives. Bayside Brews is prepared to reward your perseverance. And you can always backtrack to Pacific Wharf and wine country splendor.

*Grizzly Peak.* Another seemingly dry spot, with Smokejumpers Grill your only obvious alternative. But, as long as the Disney's Grand Californian gate remains open to non-hotel guests (not a sure thing), we have access to Hearthstone, White Water, and Napa Rose. Technically, you can pop into Storytellers Cafe, but if you are of a mind to leave a Disney park, and sit down at a Disney character restaurant just to drink, you need more help than I do.

# From Mickey and Friends Parking Structure

First, never drink and drive. This section is intended for individuals and groups who have a responsible, designated driver and currently find themselves in the parking lot in need of direction, and a drink. Perhaps you have just come out the other end of a difficult slog through traffic. Or, your drive in was seamless, but the people you are with necessitate immediate mitigation. The parking lot tram takes guests to Downtown Disney District's east end. La Brea Bakery and Naples Restaurante welcome those seeking a meal with their refreshment.

For those of a more compulsive nature, there is Napolini, or you can head straight into Disney California Adventure, if that fits the day's itinerary.

For the wholly impatient, from the parking structure, the Disneyland Hotel may be reached on foot. It's not exactly adjacent, but it could take less time than waiting for the tram, and might provide the perfect excuse for dividing up your party in a pinch. Absolutely reconsider your friendship with anyone who would rather wait for a shuttle, over joining you in a brisk walk and a Dole Whip Rum Cocktail.

# From Downtown Disney Area Parking

If you use valet, I commend you on your obvious good fortune. You are to be congratulated, also, as from the valet stand you are mere feet away from a dozen bars, and by the nature of what you've just done, you are no longer responsible for your car.

Until Disney changes its policy, Downtown Disney self-parking presents an interesting option for drinkers. First, do not even consider the following advice unless you have a designated driver. Second, this only works if your designated driver is an eager pedestrian, and your entire group agrees they would rather pay for beer, and not parking.

At press time, you can park at the west end of Downtown Disney for two hours, for free. Your group can get almost anywhere in Downtown Disney, or any of the Disney Resort hotels, and get a drink well within two hours. You will be amazed at how quickly that window closes.

Make sure your driver knows what they're in for. If they decide mid-explanation that they aren't on board, this whole thing falls apart. You could wind up blowing your beer money on parking, taxis, and a lot of stuff for which you hadn't budgeted.

Here's the rub. Someone sober needs to move the car before the two hours expire. You don't simply get to move to an alternate parking spot. You have to leave the lot, then come back in and get a new ticket. This restarts the 2-hour clock. If you have a friend who is willing to do this more than once, while the rest of you sit at the Uva bar getting intoxicated, I want to become your friend, so you can introduce me to that friend.

# CHAPTER NINE

# Disney California Adventure Drinking Game

At Walt Disney World, in Epcot specifically, locals, annual passholders, semi-regulars, and ambitious off-duty cast members carry on a dubious tradition know as Drinking Around the World. An incredible endeavor, if you can conduct yourself responsibly. Given that it is essentially an elaborate alcohol consumption competition, responsible behavior disqualifies you from the event. The activity itself, then, is tainted by its very nature.

The object of Drinking Around the World is to consume one culturally distinct adult beverage from each of Epcot's eleven international pavilions around the World Showcase. It means twelve drinks in one visit, if you include the African Outpost, which you should, since they sell alcohol.

*Disclaimer:* no one should truly participate in this reckless pursuit. Twelve drinks ought to cover a person for an extended weekend. Attempting to drink that much in a single Disney day is shameful, and a violation of that which the entire glorious resort represents. Getting truly drunk at Walt Disney World only detracts from your experience, and potentially that of anyone you encounter that day. Yes, there is a wealth of alcoholic outlets and options. No, they do not all require your custom. Certainly not all at once.

A variation of this questionable pursuit has evolved at the Disneyland Resort. Enthusiastic, if twisted Disney California Adventure visitors have conceived of a quest circumnavigating the park, snatching up drinks at every onsite alcohol vendor. Crazy? It's unthinkable.

Like its Walt Disney World counterpart, not only is this adventure outrageously expensive, it necessitates a personal and social abandon incompatible with a Disney park, the Walt Disney Company, and the very memory of Walt Disney himself.

For those guests who might be interested in Drinking Around California, say, over the course of a year, I present the specific details below. For any keen on the one-day death march, rather, I direct you to seek professional counseling.

## The Rules

From the Disney California Adventure front gate, proceed around the park in an intentionally clockwise manner. The park does not trace a pure circle, and you are going to have to crisscross and backtrack occasionally to complete a full circuit. To most simply accomplish the mission, go left at every crossroads, favoring what qualifies as the main road as much as it is available.

Your first beverage stop, along Buena Vista Street, is Carthay Circle. This is also the first point of contention for disparate Drinking Around California participants. Purists claim we ought to bear left at the first open pathway, slightly before Carthay Circle, into Hollywood Land. That would make Award Wieners the first stop. If you don't hit spots as you pass within sight of them, you are going to have to double back, a lot. You shouldn't do this at all, but for the sake of having the details down, the Carthay Circle method is simpler and better.

The object, then, is to order an adult beverage of your choice. Consume it, then continue primarily clockwise, on down to the next stop. Award Wieners is next, unless you went there first. If you did, you now have to decide whether to go back to Carthay, or head on down the line. Refer to the park map. The difficulty in catching Carthay later along the route seals the argument for those who consider it the best place to start.

If Studio Specialties is open, it is your third stop. If it is not, you get to enjoy a nice leisurely stroll with your Karl Strauss Red Trolley Ale, Award Wiener's only adult beverage offering. The walk through "a bug's land", where there is no alcohol, to Cars Land, where there is plenty, ought to be where it occurs to you to quit this outrageousness. In just over 30 minutes you've managed to drop nearly $40, and you've accomplished nothing. Well, you did see Carthay Circle, which is charming. However, you subsequently shrouded the experience in several layers of fermented sugar, which will make everything else you do difficult to remember.

When common sense, distance, drunkenness, and financial peril fail to prevail upon you to stop, participants do enter a wholly wonderful segment of the game. In Cars Land, Fillmore's Pomegranate Limeade and Racer 5 IPA await, at the Cozy Cone Motel and Flo's Café, respectively. Delightful enough to be your first and only two stops on the California drinking tour, if you are determined to go on, you have another difficult choice to make.

Maintaining clockwise momentum carries the unrelenting through Radiator Springs into the back entrance to Pacific Wharf. Here one faces four beverage stations within one square acre of patio. If you insist upon carrying on with the drinking tour of California, this is where you need to re-evaluate your life choices, and your reasons for being at a family fun park. Two of the drink options are wonderful: Karl Strauss craft beer and Rita's Grand Margaritas. If you even contemplate drinking at these, and Lucky Fortune Cookie, and Cocina Cucumunga, in succession, after hitting all the previous spots, promptly escort yourself out of the park.

At this point in the game, you're wasting quality beer, in addition to the memorable fun you should be having at the Disneyland Resort. Nine drinks in, and you haven't even covered one half of this single park. Get ahold of yourself. Quit drinking and go on some rides. Probably better make it something tame. You are pushing double-digit cocktails, and Drinking Around California knuckleheads tend not to eat properly.

If accurately following these directions, all but our instruction to cease and desist, you're right across from Ariel's Undersea Adventure. Go ride that seven or eight times. Then, find a bench, sit, and eat all the popcorn you can get your hands on. Have someone you trust escort you somewhere safe to sleep it off.

I will continue with the rules of the game, assuming everyone following along is doing so for entertainment only. That, or you have the sense to break this all up over the course of several visits.

We left off with you drifting into unconsciousness on Pacific Wharf. Hopefully, this is an entirely different day, and you again have your wits about you. Next on the route are the glorious wine terraces. It would be a shame to be here in an unappreciative state.

Mendocino and Sonoma and Alfresco Tasting Terrace occupy a spectacular section of park, and you want to be mostly sober to enjoy it, at least at first. Part of the fun of this contest is to try different drinks. Here's your opportunity to have some wonderful wine. Get something you've never heard of, if you can. Each terrace does serve beer, but if you can stand in the midst of such glory, and order a Miller Light, well, just don't.

Alfresco is not always open. If it's not, you miss a glorious spot to enjoy a glass of bliss. It is one less drink with which to poison yourself, if you're still bent on drinking your way around the park. So, there's that.

Whichever order you visit the terraces, your next move is to cross over into Paradise Pier. The Cove Bar should be your next stop. Veterans of the Cove Bar are now knowingly shaking their heads. Time was when you could walk up, take your pick of tables, or a seat at the bar, and enjoy the wide-open splendor. What happens now: you get to queue up with a hundred other people and wait for an overwrought, poorly treated hostess to try to shoehorn you in amidst the fighting families and inconsiderate freeloaders who absolutely refuse to leave.

If you have the patience, and if you get in, here is your opportunity to sample from the Disneyland Resort specialty cocktails menu. You've just had wine, and there are other outlets for fantastic beer, so jump on something colorful with a bunch of ingredients you'd otherwise never think to combine in your body.

I know mojitos are so 2012, but there's this Raspberry-Ginger Vojito that is just exciting and different enough to be worth a shot. It's as sweet as the dessert you will no longer need, and again, should be your final drink of the night.

But, not you. You are determined to press on. Just know, even if you did spread this madness over multiple days, the next part of the game is still going to kill you.

At the far extent of Paradise Pier is a lovely dining pavilion. The dining options are exquisite, there is often live entertainment, and each of the three eateries sell beer. While it doesn't seem to present the hazards of the Pacific Wharf patio, with four beverage dispensaries of its own, that was fully four drinks ago.

Bayside Brews is just waiting to entice you with a weighty, delicious beer. On the heels of three wines and a multi-layered specialty cocktail, a high ABV brew should do you in.

Excellent news: there is only one drink left. The other really good news that could well save your life: it's really far away from here. Back through Grizzly Peak, almost all the way back to the gate, Smokejumpers Grill is the last remaining pin in the map.

You may as well get the sangria. What are you saving yourself for at this point, anyway? In that vein, grab a corn dog and an espresso along the way, and go on Grizzly River Run. Now do you agree with us what a bad idea Drinking Around California is?

Drinking multiple, disparate, culturally thrilling beverages around Epcot's beautiful World Showcase Lagoon can be an incredible experience, if you do it responsibly, mostly sharing your drink, and absolutely not doing it as part of one of those drinking clubs Disney surely hopes become a thing of the past. Trying to engage in a similar activity at Disney California Adventure carries neither the cultural fulfillment nor any admirable sense of purpose.

Drinking Around California is a cry for help. It is an activity absolutely and completely unsuited to where it takes place. If your day is going to involve compulsive drinking, and you feel it should also include Disney, stay home, open a bottle of whatever, and rent the *Toy Story* trilogy.

# Last Call

Enjoy Disneyland Resort for all its worth. Go on rides. Stay with your family. Eat fried dough, and absolutely make time for adult pursuits. Disney wouldn't sell alcohol if they didn't want you to drink it (or if it wasn't such a prolific money-maker). A drink or two within the confines of your visit often adds an extra layer of euphoria to a glorious Disney experience. Stay in control, keep your fun clean, mostly, and keep your influence on strangers to a minimum. Leave the excessive volume and rash behavior to the Abominable Snowman and the little monsters in Toontown.

A perfect Disney day only requires one to follow a very simple recipe: an open mind, childlike enthusiasm, bright yellow popcorn, a ride on one or more of the "mountains," and a local vino or IPA. Combine in any order and let Disneyland handle the rest. Enjoy responsibly. Make memories you can cherish, and I'll look for you on the terrace.

# Acknowledgments

I enthusiastically thank my loving parents, Elisabeth and Dennis, who implanted, nurtured, and taught me to harvest my Disney passion. Recently, after several decades of not being at Disneyland together, they made the observation that from anywhere in the park, I know exactly where to find the closest bathroom. I take that for the profound compliment as it is intended.

I thank Paul Barre who introduced me to Napa Rose, and the cast-member wonder that is Joe.

I thank Megan and Ned Biehl who throw an incredible Complete Guide to runDisney party, and taught me that gin drinking is not inherently disreputable. I was just drinking the wrong gin.

I shall acknowledge English colonialism for the eventual development of India Pale Ale, and I thank Karl Strauss and Ballast Point for their specific, wonderful means of brewing it.

# About the Author

Christopher Schmidt is a former Disneyland Resort bartender and author of *The Complete Guide to runDisney: Disneyland Edition* (Theme Park Press). If it involves amusement, attractions, athletics, adventure, and responsible enjoyment of exotic libations, you will find Christopher in the middle of it, eager to write and tell you all about it.

# ABOUT THEME PARK PRESS

Theme Park Press publishes books primarily about the Disney company, its history, culture, films, animation, and theme parks, as well as theme parks in general.

Our authors include noted historians, animators, Imagineers, and experts in the theme park industry.

We also publish many books by first-time authors, with topics ranging from fiction to theme park guides.

And we're always looking for new talent. If you'd like to write for us, or if you're interested in the many other titles in our catalog, please visit:

www.ThemeParkPress.com

• • • • • • • • • • • • • • • • • • • • • • • • • • • • • • • • • • • • •

## Theme Park Press Newsletter

Subscribe to our free email newsletter and enjoy:

- ◆ Free book downloads and giveaways
- ◆ Access to excerpts from our many books
- ◆ Announcements of forthcoming releases
- ◆ Exclusive additional content and chapters
- ◆ And more good stuff available nowhere else

To subscribe, visit www.ThemeParkPress.com, or send email to newsletter@themeparkpress.com.

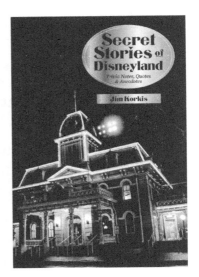

Read more about these books
and our many other titles at:

**www.ThemeParkPress.com**